W9-AQP-359

THE BEST OF BRANN

THE ICONOCLAST

SELECTED ARTICLES

Edited by
ROGER N. CONGER

Library of Congress Catalog Card Number
67 - 27148

Published by

Waco, Texas

Binding by
Library Binding Co.
Waco, Texas

A Foreword

by Roger N. Conger

The surname Brann is itself a rather uncommon one. In America, at least, the family has never been abundant. And the one who in all likelihood attained for it the widest renown, or perhaps notoriety, was the gifted, eccentric journalist of the eighteen-nineties named William Cowper Brann—better known, among most, as Brann The Iconoclast.

An Iconoclast, according to Webster, is someone who attacks cherished ideals, as shams or falsehoods. W. C. Brann fixed upon the word, out of the bottomless depths of his vocabulary, as the appropriate title for his personal "periodical of protest," an inoffensive-appearing little pulp magazine which he launched at Austin, Texas, in 1891. The journal attracted admirers, but in numbers insufficient to keep it long afloat. In about a year Brann abandoned this first attempt, and was able to dispose of his press and fixtures to an Austin friend and fellow scribe named Sidney Porter, later famed as "O'Henry."

In 1894 when Brann had moved to Waco, the home of Baptist Baylor University and for years renowned as "the Athens of Texas," he tried it once again. And this time the outcome was far different, due, very likely, to lessons gained from the earlier experience: *Brann's Iconoclast* was an almost immediate, and a whopping, success. Before assaying the product, let us first review the makings of the producer.

W. C. Brann's beginnings were classically humble. He was born in 1855 in Coles County, Illinois, to the family of a backwoods Presbyterian preacher. They named him William Cowper after the shy and ultra-sensitive British poet, and while Brann developed brilliance and even the bent to poesy, the similarity there ended.

The mother died when William was only two years old, and the father felt obliged to place the infant for rearing with some friends, a farming family named Hawkins. There is evidence that the foster parents were kind, although typically strict and straight-laced. The boy was adventurous and imaginative by nature, and when he was only thirteen, and in the third grade in country school, he slipped away one night, with his few belongings in a small carton he could carry. He was never to return, nor did he receive any further formal schooling.

Strong-willed and intelligent, he experienced little difficulty in obtaining jobs, first as a hotel bellboy, then a house-painter's helper, and, while still in his 'teens, as a "printer's devil" and cub reporter. Here he found his element. He had always loved to read, and with the opportunity to put the written word to use upon his own, literature of every kind and quality became his passion. He devoured the classics, histories of the nations and all races, mythology, and philosophy from the Greeks to Thomas Carlyle, and his powers of retention were simply prodigious.

While reporters' wages of that day were hardly generous, he doubtless sensed there were bigger things ahead, as in 1877 the youthful scribe took himself a wife, Miss Carrie Belle Martin, at Rochelle, Illinois. Their life together was unquestionably Brann's most sustaining source of enrichment, and he, in turn, was ever the exemplary, devoted husband and father. They had three children, two daughters, Inez and Grace, and a son, Bill. In 1890 there occurred a tragedy which shadowed Brann's life and outlook: his daughter Inez, then twelve, took her own life by poisoning, over an emotional quarrel with her parents. Brann was racked by a sense of guilt in the matter, and was only barely able to recover his own perspective and equilibrium.

By 1883 the breezy young reporter was promoted into the field of feature story and editorial composition, and from the first it was keenly apparent that he was possessed of a unique talent. His folksy style, and manipulation of words, earned him an appreciative following. At the same time, his acidity, and his perpetual inclination to stinging criticism, frequently embroiled his papers and their publishers in serious and at times expensive controversy. He was too frequently called upon the carpet by his superiors, and it doubtless was for this reason that he began quite early to consider the possibility of a publication of his very own. It was not a unique idea, of course. At St. Louis, the brainy esthete William Marion Reedy was putting out his *Mirror*. Elbert Hubbard, of the long hair and Windsor tie, published *The Philistine: A Periodical of Protest*, at his celebrated East Aurora, New York. At Houston, Texas, "K. Lamity" Bonner was printing *The Harpoon*, with its masthead credo—"Minnows Are Safe—We Are After Whales." And there were others. Someone has described it as the day of the "fighting pamphleteer," and this was true. They had an eager, clamorous clientele. Daily newspapers were just coming into being, and the public was hungry to keep up with events. Literature of every sort was experiencing a bonanza, and study clubs were being organized on every side. The great Victorian Era, with its false modesty and purple sentimentality, was drawing to its close, and World's Fairs and railroad excursions were bringing big-city sophistication to the perennially placid countryside. "Pagan Bob" Ingersoll had made it smart to be a doubter.

In 1886, after three highly broadening years on the St. Louis *Globe-Democrat*, Brann moved to Texas, to be editorial writer for the Galveston *Evening Tribune*. Becoming ever harder to manage or control, he changed jobs twice within the next five years, first to the rival Galveston *News*, and from there to the Houston *Post*. It was while in Houston that he lost his little Inez; and for reasons yet not fully known, he developed a fantastic aversion for the

Post editor, Rienzi M. Johnston. He referred to Johnston frequently in later years in the most caustic fashion.

Early in 1891 he moved to Austin, and it was here that, staking all his necessarily limited savings, he launched the first issue of his dream-sheet, *The Austin Iconoclast.* Its failure to attain an adequate momentum was a blow to the author's pride. But he had a family to think about, and was able to salvage some of his investment before returning to newspaper employment as of yore. He went back briefly to St. Louis, and then returned to Texas for the San Antonio *Express.* At San Antonio he added considerably to his fame as a gad-fly, and kept the *Express* in one scrape after another. It was in November, 1894, that he moved to Waco, in Central Texas, ostensibly as chief editorialist for the Waco *Daily News.* Undoubtedly he had with him a bulging file of his explosive essays, crying for publication. In cooperation with a courageous Waco printer, in February, 1895, he blasted the newsstands and railroad trains with the first issue of the new *Iconoclast.*

The writing style was absolutely unique—an imaginative blending of the beautiful with the banal and barbaric, nearly poetic tenderness with cow-lot crudity, supported throughout by lightning flashes of original thought, philosophy, and wit. The public went perfectly wild about it. And within no more than five or six months, Brann's future, and that of his hypnotic little magazine, were at last solidly assured. Having battled upward to independence as he had, it must have been a victory of incomparable sweetness. The sweetness did not, however, permeate through to his pen.

In the first issue at Waco, the author affirmed that he was not hoping to "reform the world" or to "drag the golden age in by the ears, or pull the millenium before it is ripe." He proposed only to "recover a few acres of Mother Earth from the domain of Falsehood and Folly."

Back at St. Louis, Brann had learned an important point from the *Globe-Democrat* editor, J. B. McCullagh. While no brawler himself, McCullagh had once commented to Brann, "When you have to go after a man, put a drop of vitriol on him. Don't pour a barrel of vinegar over him." Brann was never low on vitriol.

He nurtured a number of seemingly especial aversions, for reasons frequently known only to himself. High upon such a list were Baptists, in general. Brann said he didn't believe they'd been held under water long *enough;* and he scourged Baylor University as "that great storm-center of misinformation."

Another fanatical dislike was the British—the people, or anything concerning them. When an editorial in a British newspaper aroused his ire, he roared that "Uncle Sam should once again take old John Bull by the collar and drive the toe of his boot so far underneath his coat tails the pompous fraud would taste leather for a year."

Perhaps his harshest approach was bestowed upon the Negro. It is difficult to analyze the depth of this bitterness, which was always caustic and frequently brutal and inflammatory. In one essay he remarked that "the Negro is to the American social organism what a pound of putty would be in the stomach of a dyspeptic." Again, in an essay attacking the churches' Foreign Mission programs, he expressed this opinion—"Everywhere [in America] the widow is battling want, while these Pharisees send Bibles and blankets, salvation and missionary soup to a job-lot of lazy niggers, whose souls ain't worth a sou-markee in blocks of five—who wouldn't walk into Heaven if the gates were wide open, but once inside would steal the eternal throne if it wasn't spiked down."

Toward women his references were invariably chivalrous and idealistic. But he considered them intellectually inferior, and had no sympathy for the contemporary movement to grant to them more equal privileges. In Brann's opinion "the average woman would rather have one baby than forty ballots. Give to a woman youth and beauty and she asks not, needs not political power. But when, still a maid, her mirror tells her she could not pass for five-and-forty in the moonlight . . . she declines to endure the ills she has, but flies to others she knows not of."

Prohibition was another topic of divisive controversy, and concerning it Brann wrote, "I do not oppose prohibition because I am the friend of liquor, but because I am the friend of liberty. I would rather see a few boozers than a race of bondmen."

As is most highly apparent, he was never undecided, never neutral, on any subject of public interest or importance. Such a man and publisher numbered countless admirers, from far and near. One of Brann's most valued personal friends was County Judge G. B. Gerald of Waco, a highly colorful character in his own right. A capable writer himself, Judge Gerald was the very epitome of the fire-eating ex-Confederate, "jealous in honor," and "sudden and quick in quarrel."

Needless to recite, Brann and his *Iconoclast* had a full share of equally fanatic enemies and detractors. And when the vilification of Baylor University became absolutely intolerable, the once friendly little city found itself rent into two armed camps, with both sides breathing violence and practicing with pistols. As shocked citizens said about it later, something just had to happen. And something did.

It happened first between Judge Gerald and the two Harris brothers, Jim and Bill, both of the latter on the Baylor side, and both associated with the Waco *Times-Herald*. It was a brand new venture, and Jim Harris was the editor.

Judge Gerald had openly espoused the side of Brann, and had published several "open letters," in one of which he had called a prominent Waco minister "a saintly psalm-singing son of a bitch." On November 19th, 1897, at about noon, the adversaries met in a smoking three-way duel on Waco's busiest street, in which both Harrises died and the Judge lost an arm.

The violent episode seemed temporarily to restore a semblance of sanity. But the grand finale was to be not long stayed. In the late afternoon of April 1st, 1898, Brann was just leaving the city, with his business manager Bill Ward, to make a lecture tour, when a brooding supporter of Baylor named Tom Davis stepped out behind them from the doorway of a sidewalk office, and shot Brann between the shoulder blades with a heavy caliber Colt revolver. While the slug was to be fatal, Brann himself was able to wheel, draw his own gun and return the fire, with equally fatal effect. By the next day both were dead. Brann's funeral procession, at Waco, was the longest in the city's history.

Judge Gerald tried stubbornly to keep the *Iconoclast* going, largely due to his friendship for the family. But without W. C. Brann's riposting sword it faded fast, and before the same year's end was abandoned.

From across the whole country laudatory articles and obituaries compared Brann to Thomas Paine, Voltaire, Ambrose Bierce, and other immortals. Elbert Hubbard mourned that "The hand which wrote the most Carlylean phrase of any in America is cold and stiff. That soul through which surged thought too great for speech has gone a-journeying. Brann shook his cap, flourished his bauble, gave a toss to that fine head, and with tongue in cheek, asked questions and propounded conundrums that Stupid Hypocrisy could not answer."

Whatever was his stature, he cut a brief but meteoric path.

Table of Contents

Illustrations

Following Page 68

THE BEST OF BRANN

HONESTY VS. LAW

This essay, brief but breezy and pungent, appeared in May, 1895. It well represents, in thumbnail fashion, Brann's stiletto style.

Many men are "legally honest" who are morally rotten—conform to the statutes simply to keep out of prison. Legal honesty is the brand usually proclaimed as "the best policy." Only fools risk the penitentiary to fill their purse; the smart rascal is ever honest with the law—infamous in strict accord with the criminal code. The man once declared a bankrupt may become a multi-millionaire, see people he settled with at 15 cents on the dollar die in the poor house, decline to pay them their just dues, and still be legally honest; but if you lend him a chew o' tobacco you had best take a receipt for it.

* * *

Dives may attire himself in purple and fine linen and fare sumptuously every day, while Lazarus lies at his door for the dogs to lick, vainly craving the crumbs that fall from his table, and still be well within the law—even a church member in good standing; but his loyalty to legal forms will avail him but little when he finds his shirt-tail afire and no water within 40 miles.

* * *

The girl who flirts with a featherless young gosling until he doesn't know whether he's floating in a sea of champagne to the sound of celestial music, sliding down a greased rainbow, or riding on the ridge-pole of the Aurora Borealis, then tells him she can only be a Christmas-present-opera-ticket sister to him; who steals his unripe affections and allows 'em to get frost-bitten—carries him into the empyrean of puppy love only to drop him with a dull plunk that fills his callow heart with compound fractures—well, she cannot be prosecuted for petty larceny nor indicted for malicious mischief; but the unfortunate fellow who finally gets her will be glad to go to heaven, where there's neither marrying nor giving in marriage.

* * *

The man who preaches prohibition in public and pays court to a gallon jug of corn-juice in private; who damns the saloon at home and sits up with it all night abroad, may not transcend the law of the land; but if the Lord wants him the devil will discount his claim.

* * *

The man who sues a fellow citizen for "alienating his wife's affections," instead of striking his trail with a bell-mouthed blunderbuss and a muzzle loading bull dog; who asks the court to put a silver lining in the cloud of infamy that hangs over his home—tries to make capital of his shame and heal with golden guineas the hurt that honor feels—even he may be a "law-abiding citizen," but ten thousand such souls might play hide-and-seek on the surface of a copper cent for a hundred years and never find each other.

* * *

The little tin-horn attorney, whose specialties are divorce cases and libel suits; who's ever striving to stir up good-for-naughts to sue publishers of newspapers for $10,000 damages to 10-cent reputations; who's as ready to shield Vice from the sword of Justice as to defend Virtue from stupid Violence; who is ever for sale to the highest bidder—keeps tears on tap for whosoever will drop a dollar in the slot; will weep over the woes of the red-handed homicide or bewail the gaping wounds of his victim; will take a contingent fee to bleed his best friend, or enter into a conspiracy to despoil honest industry by due process of law; will rob the orphan of his patrimony on a legal technicality and brand the Virgin Mary as a bawd to shield a blackmailer—well, he can't be put in the penitentiary, more's the pity! but it's some satisfaction to believe that if, in all the great universe of God there is a hell where fiends lie howling, the most sulphurous section is reserved for the infamous shyster, the carrion crow of human kind—that if he cannot be debarred from the courts of earth he'll get the bounce from those of heaven.

FACT AND FANCY
Dished Up in Broken Doses

In the following article, the author permits himself a little more philosophy and a little less of spleen.

Truth and only Truth is eternal. It was not born and it cannot die. It may be obscured by the clouds of Falsehood, or buried in the debris of brutish Ignorance, but it can never be destroyed. It's all that is, or was, or can ever be. It exists in every atom, lives in every flower and flames in every star. When the heavens and the earth shall pass away, and the universe return to cosmic dust, divine Truth alone will stand unscathed amid the crash of matter and the wreck of worlds. Falsehood is an amorphous monster, conceived in the brain of knaves and brought forth by the breath of fools. It's a moral pestilence, a miasmic vapor that passes like a blast from hell over the face of the world, and is gone forever. It may leave death in its wake and disaster dire; it may place on the brow of purity the brand of the courtesan and cover the hero with the stigma of the coward; it may degrade the patriot and exalt the demagogue, enslave an Horatio and crown a Humbug; it may wreck hopes and ruin homes, cause blood to flow and hearts to break; it may pollute the altar and disgrace the throne, corrupt the courts and curse the land; but the lie cannot live forever; and when it's dead and damned there's none so poor as to do it reverence.

* * *

Print the grandest sermon that ever fell from Massillon's lips of gold, and not 20 per cent, even of the professedly pious, will read it; print a detailed account of an international prize fight and 99 per cent of the very elect will make a dive for the paper before breakfast,—will swoop down upon it like a hungry hen-hawk reaching for an unripe gosling and fairly devour it, then roll their eyes to heaven like a calf with the colic and wonder what this wicked old world is coming to.

* * *

We pore over books too much and reflect too little, depend too much on others, too little upon ourselves. We make of our heads cold-storage warehouses for other people's ideas, instead of standing up in our own independent, God-like individuality. Reading is the nurse of culture, reflection the mother of genius. Our great religions were born in the desert; our grandest philosophies budded and burgeoned in the wilderness; the noblest poesy that ever swept the human harpischord was born in the brain of a beggar, came bubbling from the heart of the blind; and when all the magi of the Medes, and all the great philosophers of Greece had failed to furnish forth a jurisprudence just to all, semi-barbarous Rome laid down those laws by which, even from the grave of her glory, she still rules the majestic world.

Our educational system is Procrustean. It magnifies the mesquite but mangles the Cedars of Lebanon; runs a Burke and a blockhead, a Johnson and a jacksnipe thro' the same mill,—the intellectual pismire and the mental Colossus thro' the same curriculum.

* * *

I always feel sorry for the man who's got nothing to be proud of but a dead gran'daddy, for it appears to be a law of nature that there shall be but one great man to a tribe,—that the lightning of genius shall not twice strike the same family tree. Talent may be transmitted from father to son; but you can no more inherit genius than you can inherit a fall out of a balloon. It is a direct gift of that God who is no respecter of persons, and who sheds his glory on the cotter's child as freely as upon those of monarchs and of millionaires.

* * *

We have in this country three aristocracies: The aristocracy of intellect, founded by the Almighty; the aristocracy of money, founded by Mammon; and the aristocracy of family, founded by fools. To the first belonged Abraham Lincoln, and his title was as good while swinging the ox-goad as while breaking the fetters of the blacks. The colossal figure was there, tho' obscured by the shadows. The nation burst into flame, and the Titan was outlined against the lurid sky. Had the volcano slumbered on, Lincoln might have lived unknown and died unwept by the great world,—one of the many village Hampdens, or mute, inglorious Miltons.

* * *

Love is the most sacred word ever framed by celestial lips. It embraces all that is holy in human life, every gleam of supernal glory that radiates from the immaculate throne of the Infinite. Of Love was born every grace and beauty in heaven and earth, every holy aspiration, every hope of immortality. It out-ranks every religion, is above and beyond all that human hand ever penned on papyrus or graved on stone, superior to the dust of dead prophets and the uncertain voice of departed priests; for it's the law of Life, the harmony of Heaven, the breath of which the universe was born,—the Divine Essence increate of the ever-living God.

* * *

The place to take the true measure of a man is not the forum or the field, not the market-place or the amen-corner, but at his own fireside. There he lays aside his mask and you may judge whether he's imp or angel, king or cur, hero or humbug. I care not what the world says of him,—whether it crown him with bays or pelt him with bad eggs; I care never a copper what his reputation or religion may be: If his babes dread his home-coming and his better half swallows her heart every time she has to ask him for a five-dollar bill, he's a fraud of the first water, even tho' he prays night and morn till he's black in the face, and howls hallelujah till he shakes the eternal hills. But if his children rush to the front gate to greet him, and love's own sunshine illumes the face of his wife when she hears his footfall, you may take it for granted that he's true gold, for his home's a heaven and the humbug never gets that near the great white throne of God. He may be a rank atheist and a redflag anarchist, a Mormon and a Mugwump; he may buy votes in blocks of five and bet on the election; he may deal 'em from the bottom of the deck and drink beer till he can't tell a silver dollar from a circular saw, and still be an infinitely better man than the cowardly little hypocrite who is all suavity in society, yet makes his home a hell,—who vents upon the hapless heads of wife and children the ill-nature he would like to inflict upon his fellow men, but dares not. I can forgive much in that fellow mortal who would rather make men swear than women weep; who would rather have the hate of the whole he-world than the contempt of his wife,—who would rather call anger to the eyes of a king than fear to the face of a child.

THE HEROES OF HISTORY

Here is the scholar parading the great names of history, but yielding the greener laurels to those unsung.

Many of the martyrs whose memories we revere, of the saints we apotheosize, of the heroes we enshrine in history, were one-third fraud and two-thirds fake. The man who can grow in grace while his pet corn's in chancery, or lose an election without spraining his moral character; who can wait an hour for his dinner without walking all over the nerves of his wife, or crawl out of bed in the middle of his first nap and rustle till the cold, gray dawn with a brace of colicky kids, without broadly insinuating that he was a copper-riveted, nickel-plated, automatic, double-cylinder idiot ever to get married, is a greater hero than he that taketh a city.

* * *

The hero is not he that strives with the world for witness, who seeks the bubble fame at the cannon's brazen throat, and risks his life that he may live forever.

> "Think not that helm and harness are signs of valor true;
> Peace hath higher tests of manhood than battles ever knew."

To bear with becoming grace the slings and arrows of outrageous fortune; to find our heaven in others' happiness and for their sake to sacrifice, and suffer wrongs that might be righted with a thread of steel; to live an honest life in a land where Truth doth feed on crusts, while Falsehood fattens at Lucullean feasts, requires more moral stamina, more true manliness than to follow a flag into the very jaws of hell, or die for the faith in the *auto da fe.*

* * *

Why unurn the ashes of the half-forgotten dead, and pore o'er the musty pages of the past for names to glorify? If you would find heroes grander, martyrs more noble and saints of more sanctity than a Rubens ever painted or immortal Homer sang; who, without Achilles' armor have slain an hundred Hectors, without Samsonian locks have torn the lion, without the sword of Michael have thrown down the gage to all the embattled hosts of hell, seek not in the musty tomes of history, but in the hearts and homes of the self-sacrificing wives and mothers of this great world.

* * *

Let the heroes of history have their due; still I imagine the world will have been much the same had Alexander died of cholera infantum or grown up a harmless dude. I don't think the earth unbalanced would from its orbit fly had Caesar been drowned in the Rubicon or Jim Corbett never been born. I imagine that Greece would have humbled the Persian's pride had there been no Thermopylae, that Rome would have ruled the world had Scaevola's good right hand not hissed in the Tuscan fire. One catfish does not make a creek, nor one hero a nation. The waves do not make the sea, but the sea furnishes forth the waves. Leonidas were lost to history but for the three hundred nameless braves who backed his bluff; had there been but one Cromwell, Charles the First would have kept his head; in Washington's deathless splendor gleams the glory of forgotten millions, and the history of Bonaparte is written in the blood of the unknown brave.

A TOUCH OF HIGH LIFE

The Press and the Parvenues

Brann here amply airs his immoderate contempt for the contemporary Jet Set.

There was a time when the principal business of the American press was the publication of important news and the expression of opinion anent matters of moment. In those days it posed as a "public educator," and the self-bestowed title was not altogether inappropriate; but it has, for the most part, dropped its high pretensions and is now notoriously "out for the stuff." The "great dailies" that once went in for glory and aspired to decency, that "molded public opinion" and "saved the country" semi-occasionally, are not averse to accepting a fat fee for championing some particular interest, regardless of the general welfare. When it was proven that the *Galveston-Dallas News* had sold its alleged editorial influence, it had the audacity to defend the practice as legitimate journalism! A majority of the other morning papers of Texas are not of sufficient importance to justify the public in keeping tab on them. If they should succeed in selling their souls for a copper cent the public would only pity the purchaser. When the great dailies are not "pulling the leg" of some corporation with a legislative axe to grind, or inflating with a pneumogastric bellows some political boomlet born of a bank account, they are courting the parvenues—who are every ready to pay for publicity—puffing society belles for a consideration, obsequiously bowing to cymling-headed dudes with more dollars than sense and gathering in the golden shekels from every available source.

The marriage of Miss Anna Gould—a very commonplace young person—to a French butterfly whom we have no evidence ever did aught to entitle him to existence upon the earth, afforded the "independent" American press an opportunity to slop over in great shape, and it slopped. Tons of toads were eaten with evident relish, fulsome flattery fairly overran the column rules, and the disgusting tide of eulogistic dish water is now but slowly ebbing.

Some of the bridegroom's ancestors had once borne petty titles—out of which the *tiers etat* unceremoniously kicked the sawdust; but the nice little thing, who is of less importance to the world at large than a blind wiggletail, still clings to his title like a spendthrift to a canceled pawn ticket—calls himself the "Count de Castellane"—and spends his time painting, primping and puttering about like a girl inoculated with the matrimonial itch. And the great American dailies, which are supposed to be the very avatars of rugged republicanism, "dearly love a lord" even tho' his title be worth no more than a draft on a broken bank or a cook book to a starving hobo. Miss Gould was the rather stupid daughter of an American sovereign who began life as a map-maker and mouse-trap architect, and who succeeded, by very questionable methods, in amassing an enormous fortune. "Nobility and wealth!" That were indeed a combination sufficient to cause the average American editor to bow his face to the earth and lick boots until he resembled a tame duck with its mouth full of dried mud! The great dailies informed us when the little "Count" went to bed and when he got up. They told us what he ate for breakfast and how he spent each day, but even "journalistic enterprise" could not catch him in the water closet. The press watched the little parvenue who had purchased him as narrowly as a hungry buzzard could a spoiled beefsteak. "It was a love match, pure and simple," they informed the world—then wondered in the next paragraph if she would utilize the trousseau purchased less than a year ago, when she was engaged to wed some other gilly. But she didn't. She could afford a new one—the mouse-trap of her sire had been set for suckers as well as for ravenous rodentia. The trousseau purchased when she made that other "love match, pure and simple," was not nearly good enough in which to be tied fast to a titled dude—like a living man to a dead mule. The cable was kept hot ordering new "dreams of loveliness" from the he-milliners and mustachioed mantua-makers of "Paree," and the great dailies had to tell us all about it—just how each gown was cut and what it cost, how many suits of silk lingerie the bride-elect had ordered and their colors. Whether the "Count" ordered any extra underwear for the occasion the newspapers neglected to state, which omission leads us to suspect that he was not addicted to the luxury of lingerie and the expense of pajamas before he succeeded in trading his Confederate bond title and mortgaged chateau for fifteen millions of Jay Gould's ill-got gold. The Associated Press—the champion toad-eater of the universe—informed us, however, that before ze "Count" could obtain a special dispensation from his theological boss to bag the eager heiress she had to sign an agreement not to inferfere with the religious faith of Frenchy and consent that their kids be brought up Roman Catholics. If His Holiness had but seen his niblets he would probably have considered the latter stipulation entirely unnecessary—a work of supererogation, so to speak. In about two years we may expect to see the "Countess" come sneaking back to her own countree in company with a divorce case and a tale of woe that would wring the briny from a bust of Sitting Bull. It is the usual way. She will have the experience, the "Count" will have the cash and the newspapers will have another scandal with whiskers on it that trail the shrinking earth.

* * *

In the hurly-burly of getting Miss Gould married, the newspapers rather neglected the divorce case of Mr. and Mrs. Willie K. Vanderbilt—only giving us a column or so each day as condiment. But they had been hammering at it for lo! these many moons—had already told us, several times, all they knew about it and pretty much everything that a morbid imagination could guess at. Willie and his wife separated some time ago for reasons which they succeeded in keeping within the sacred Vanderbiltian circle. It was known that Willie resembled Solomon in that he "loved many strange women," and that was usually supposed to constitute the *casus belli;* but Mrs. Willie did not trot to any alarming extent in the same class with Caesar's wife. That they quarreled and fought like some drunken "canary" and his drab was understood; but, by a liberal use of money they kept the divorce proceedings out of the papers, so it is not generally known whether the separation was caused by "incompatibility of temper" or mutual fornication. The pot probably grew aweary of calling the kettle black, and the latter of animadverting on the complexion of its companion, so a legal separation was secured and each can now indulge in those propensities peculiar to social swelldom untrammeled by marital ties. Mrs. Vanderbilt is one of three sisters, each of whom found a husband an inconvenient handicap. Willie and his ex-wife, buoyed up by boodle, will continue to float in the *creme de la creme*—where adultery seems to be the rule and decency the exception—and the great dailies to deluge a defenseless public with highfalutin hogwash anent their most inconsequential doings, just as tho' the common people cared a tinker's dam whether Mrs. Vanderbilt was yum-yumming with Alphabet Belmont in London while Willie was dallying with the Neustetter *nymph du pave* in Paris. Cornelius Vanderbilt, a cross-grained old curmudgeon with his bump of acquisitiveness abnormally developed, went into business and prospered. Had he failed the great dailies would trouble themselves but little about his descendants. Those who got hanged or divorced might get a few lines gratis, the marriage and death notices would cost the usual dollar per line—set in solid nonpareil and sandwiched between market reports and pure patent medicine advertisements.

* * *

Jno. W. Mackay is said to have begun life by peddling bock beer over a pine bar. This occupation probably required intellectual effort to which he found himself unequal, for he exchanged the barkeeper's apron for the miner's overalls; the bung-starter for the quartz breaker. He was a good fellow and the Goddess of Fortune favored him. When he "struck it rich" his wife, who appears to have been general manager of a miners' hash-factory, forthwith blossomed out as a "sawsiety" butterfly. A dinner of "biled" turnips and bull beef, a calico Mother Hubbard and a red bandana had formerly been the *ultima thule* of her ambition; but with millions at her command, nothing America could produce satisfied her sybaritic tastes. She obtained an establishment in "Paree," and there she is in the habit of dispensing Lucullean luxuries to the hungry horde of high-toned hoodlums who regard a fresh-picked American parvenue as an oasis in the Sahara of semi-starvation. And the daily press, which would not have given her a two-line personal when she was slinging hash and building slumgullion, began to gush like a cask of fermenting molasses, to crawl on its belly before the Mackay millions. Mrs. Mackay could not purchase a poodle or old John cut his corns without the fact being cabled across the ocean and peddled to eager papers by the Associated Press—accompanied by the usual cackle about its own remarkable "enterprise." Finally Miss Mackay persuaded papa to purchase a little macaroni prince for her to play with, and the press proceeded to have ecstatic spasms. The "Prince and Princess Colonna" loomed up by the page in all important newspapers, accompanied by double-column before-and-after-taking portraits. More space was devoted to this foolish young female and her titled lazzarone than to all the authors and artists, inventors and educators upon the earth. One would have supposed that when, in consideration of some millions of money, the Prince Colonna consented to occupy the same bedroom with the American heiress, a new and happier era had dawned upon the human race—that the millennium was at hand. But when the Prince had wrapped his scorbutic diaphragm around a few square feeds—at his wife's expense—he became so vicious that a self-respecting dog could not have endured him, and his purchaser was compelled to turn him loose. A few months of poverty usually brings him around all right, however, and a "happy reunion" results. Colonna would rather live with his plebian wife occasionally than clean cuspidores or manipulate a hurdy-gurdy for a living. Every time the Prince patches up a truce—for the purpose of acquiring more boodle to blow in on the gamblers and courtesans of European capitals—the American people are compelled to learn all about it, else boycott the daily papers. Just how much the Dago dudelet has cost old honest John will probably never be known; but the latter has doubtless regretted a dozen times that the law does not allow him to take the scurvy scion of a titled but ignoble family out behind the wood shed and knock out his seldom brains by slugging him beneath the coat tails with a brogan built for that especial business.

* * *

As these lines are penned the readers of the daily press are getting another dose of the disreputable Mrs. J. Coleman Drayton, *nee* Astor. Old John Jacob Astor embarked in the skin business and, being an artist in that particular line, soon accumulated enough money to purchase property in Manhattan Island when it was worth about as much as a West Texas goat walk. New York grew into a great city and the "unearned increment" made the family he had incidentally founded—while trading tin tomahawks and firewater for the Aborigines' furs—as rich as a fat pork pie. Three generations have sufficed to rub the grease off his gold and transform the aggressive effluvia of his hide house into odors of Araby the Blest. J. Coleman Drayton distinguished himself by capturing one of the Astor heiresses, then started in to enjoy life regardless of expense, while the great dailies gushed and slopped, toadied and taffied. The girl was no great shakes, but her bank account was a beaut. J. Coleman was nothing to speak of, but with an Astorian fortune at his fingers' ends he quickly became an object of absorbing interest to our "public educators." But, like Othello, the gentleman who parts his name on the side and his hair in the middle became suspicious. The green-eyed monster straddled his neck, rode him around the donjon keep of the Astorian castle and permitted the portcullis to fall upon him with a dull, sodden plunk. Not caring to "keep a cistern for foul toads to knot and gender in," he gave his alleged better half the bounce. It was expected that he'd borrow an axe and carve a great three-cornered orifice in the anatomy of her paramour; but he concluded to tell his troubles to the court. An opera-bouffe duel grew out of the affair; but the cuckold was nursing his mental anguish and kept well out of the way while a brace of society swells wounded the atmosphere and attracted the world's attention to the frailties of his wife. Meanwhile the press fairly staggered beneath the burden of the sensation—a crisis seemed to have suddenly arisen in the history of the human race! We were almost led to expect that the world would cease revolving and the entire solar system slip an eccentric because a female descendant of an ignorant old fur trader had been dallying with the dudes—had strayed from home in her reckless pursuit of happiness.

And so it goes. The daily press is ever at the feet of the parvenues, always cringing before the Golden Calf. Its boasted "backbone" is made of gutta-percha, it is as deficient in moral force as a mangy yellow fice. It has degenerated from a public educator into a professional scandal-monger, from an inculcator of independent American manhood to a pitiful flunkey that serves for hire, panders to a vitiated public taste for stray pennies, flatters Mammon for its fodder and slobbers over everything with a title simply because it has no better sense. That is strong language; but it will find an echo in the heart of this mighty Yankee nation—composed, not of princes and pimps, lords and lackeys, counts and cuckolds, but of American sovereigns who do not depend upon boodle to make them respectable; who are superior, morally, mentally and physically, to the very kings of foreign countries. The proudest European nobleman is a Subject; the humblest American citizen is a Sovereign! The American who cannot understand that fact—whether "able editor" of a great daily or heiress seeking social distinction—should be castrated or killed. We are breeding entirely too many title-worshippers, toadies and intellectual tomtits—too few self-reliant, manly men, who realize that below them are all things, animate and inanimate, above them only the eternal King of kings.

THE MARLBOROUGH-VANDERBILT MARRIAGE

That the laws concerning libel were weak and ineffective in 1895 is well demonstrated in this outrageous diatribe.

The approaching marriage of Miss Consuelo Vanderbilt to the Duke of Marlborough is agitating the social world from centre to circumference. New York's Four Hundred and the fashionables of London are standing on their hind legs and wildly waving their ears. The alliance is pronounced not only "the social event of the season," but of all seasons, so far as Columbia is concerned. The capture by Miss Gould of a French count was not a circumstance to it. The Frenchman was only a count by courtesy, while the "Jook" is still doing business at Sara Jennings' old stand. The press gave us only a few columns daily anent the Gould-Castellane barter and sale, but it shoots the Vanderbilt-Marlborough affair into us by the page. The press can always be depended upon to rise equal to the occasion, and this is too evidently the supreme crisis of the universe. Millions of columns have been written anent the matter, and the deluge of intellectual bilge-water has just begun. If Heaven and Earth should again embrace to beget a second Saturnus the pencil-pushers could not be more profoundly impressed.

And who the devil are the Duke of Marlborough and Miss Vanderbilt, that the world should hold its breath while they make elaborate preparations to contribute, each to the misery of the other—to share the same bed and board? The Duke is the lineal descendants of old John Churchill and Sara Jennings, two of the most disreputable ducks that ever disgraced the earth. John utilized the virtue of his sister to break into the British "nobility," fawned at the feet of her princely paramour so long as he had power to promote his fortune, then turned traitor and sold his services to William III, by whom he was ever regarded with suspicion and treated with contempt. Like Sextus Tarquinius and Benedict Arnold, he was a soldier of some ability; but he was more shameless than the one and more corrupt than the other. Arnold would not have profited by a sister's prostitution, nor Sextus have soiled his hand with the small wage of the common soldier. John Churchill, founder of the House of Marlborough, was the Boss Tweed of his time, the prize pimp of his day and generation. As a traitor he was the peer of Judas Iscariot, and he has been equalled in shameless dishonesty only by his lineal descendants. The only assurance we have that the latter were not bastards is to be found in the fact that they were one and all stamped from head to heel with the Marlborough meanness. It is another case of the evil men do living after them, while the good is interred with their bones. Sara Jennings, his wife, was eminently worthy of so mean a mate. She was a kind of unholy cross between Xanthippe and Sycorax, the best-hated old heifer in all England. Too cold-blooded to play the prostitute herself, she was content to tend door and share in the profit of her sister-in-law's shame. The fiance of Miss Vanderbilt is descended from this impure source thro' a long line of titled cuckolds and shameless pimps, and now stands on the ragged edge of poverty, bartering to parvenues for bread an empty dukedom bought with a female relative's dishonor. The late Lord Randolph Churchill, uncle of the present duke, was unquestionably the best of the lot; but he demonstrated of what material he was made when he failed to rip the white liver out of Prince Collars and Cuffs when he caught that royal popinjay *flagrante delicto* with "Lady" Churchill, at Windsor Castle—when he accepted the foul bawd warm from the embraces of that titled nincompoop and permitted her to continue to bear his name. The father of the present duke, and his predecessor in the title was universally conceded to be the most contemptible cur in all Christendom. He had more than the vices of the original Churchill and none of his supposed virtues. He succeeded in wedding a respectable woman, but she was compelled to leave him because of his general cussedness. He then sold his title to a dizzzy New York music teacher who had managed to catch a sucker and bump his head for several millions. He ran through with Lil Hammersly's boodle, was carried to the grave with the syphilis and left a beggarly title to his particularly stupid son, who is now bartering it to the Vanderbilts.

Such, in brief, is the origin and history of "the great House of Marlborough"—a plebeian family raised to the peerage by prostitution and enriched by rascality that embraced every crime in the calendar, from petty thievery to base ingratitude, from arrant hypocrisy to high treason, to be in turn pauperized by pimps, beggared by bawds. There is not a drop of pure blood in the entire family.

There has never been one of the name entitled to be called a gentleman. The record of the house is black with more than Armenian meanness, across its escutcheon falls the bar-sinister of a woman's shame. The present duke is said to be somewhat better than his degraded progenitors. Poverty makes even dukes humble. When a "nobleman" is unable to buy so much much as a yellow pot to put in his boudoir he is apt to strike a moderate gait; but he is a Churchill, and "an evil tree cannot bring forth good fruit." In appearance, he is a tough of the toughs. He has a head like a Bowery bouncer and the mug of an ape who has met with an accident. When he gets his grip on the Vanderbilt gold it is dollars to doughnuts he will use it as did his unlamented father the millions of the gay Lil Hammersly, who paid for the privilege of being kicked and cuffed by a genuine British "nobleman" in Blenheim Palace.

And the Vanderbilts? Two hundred years ago an ignorant Hollander squatted on a patch of land at Flat Bush, L. I., and engaged in the laudable enterprise of raising cabbages, while his better half added an occasional florin to the family hoard by peddling fish. At that time the name was taken on the installment plan, being written Van Der Bilt. Old Bilt begat a son named Jacob, who followed in the footsteps of his father, and was poor without being proud. He was also a grower of cabbages, and his gude wife not above peddling sprats from door to door and filing the proceeds away in her ample yarn sock. In the course of four generations the Van Der Bilts had accumulated sufficient boodle to buy a small ferry boat, and began at once to float on to fortune. The name was coupled up to save stationery in writing it, for none realized better than they that economy is the road to wealth. By working like the Old Harry and spending never a cent, and by the rise in land values in and around New York, the Vanderbilts became wealthy enough to exchange barter in shrimps and sprats for deals in railway stocks—to purchase a coronet to offset that "very ancient and fish-like smell" which has so long clung to the descendants of old Aris. Miss Consuelo is the daughter of Wm. K. Vanderbilt, a lively old bird who was recently divorced from his wife for reasons that have been kept a family secret. It is the general impression, however, that it was a case of mutual fornication; that while "Willie" was going a rapid gait in dizzy "Paree," Alva was holding up her end of the line in London. Such is the lineage of the young lady who is about to purchase a descendant of old Judas Iscariot Churchill and Sara Jennings. She is a long, gaunt, skinny young female whose face would frighten any animal but a pauper duke out for the "dough." Her muscular arms, stub-nose and big feet proclaim her plebeian origin, while if the countenance be a true index to the intellect, she is the mental equal of a half-baked Chinese idol. If she had not been born with a silver spoon in her mouth it is doubtful if she could secure a position in the second row of the ballet on her shape, or a place in a steam laundry by her intelligence. But Miss Consuelo is an American. Were she the descendant of a Bowery tough, as homely as a hedgehog and as stupid as a Cleveland Democrat she would be infinitely too good for the best man that ever bore the title of Duke of Marlborough. We are sorry for the young lady, just as we are sorry for any calf that is being led to the shambles. She will doubtless wish a thousand times that instead of wedding the "Jooke" she had followed the example of her female ancestors—married some sturdy young Dutch farmer and peddled fish. After the glamour and glitter have worn away she will wonder if the game was worth the candle. She will look at the scorbutic subject of an old woman and compare him with the sovereigns of her native land and wish to God that she could lose him.

"What fools these mortals be"—especially where a petty title and a little money are concerned! Most of the "great American dailies" have printed pictures of the young pair who are making such elaborate preparations to occupy the same sheets; but the New York *World* out-toadies all Toadydom. It informs an alleged intelligent world just how tall Miss Vanderbilt is, the length of her foot and such other information as might be valuable were she a Papuan slave being bartered for breeding purposes. It also devotes considerable space to a description of the lingerie in which she will encase her "lithe limbs" during the honeymoon. The style is only hinted at, but we may presume that the chemise will be provided with handles and the under-garment patterned after Biela's comet or the Democratic Party. The fit will doubtless be *au fait.* The sartorial artist will doubtless be able to properly attire any portion of her anatomy by employing the *World's* measurements. We regret that our great contemporary has neglected to tell us anything about the lingerie of the bridegroom-elect. But perhaps he doesn't wear any at present. He is probably waiting for the Vanderbilt "settlement" to provide his noble anatomy with undershirts.

I wish the young turtle-doves well, but can scarce pray that their tribe may increase. I trust that having secured sufficient of the ducats hoarded up by certain Dutch fish wives to enable him to live in comfort, the duke will give us an imitation of a nobleman who is trying to be decent; that having purchased one of the two-and-twenty dukedoms of the United Kingdom, the young woman will not pattern after her giddy aunt and hang on princes' favors to the dishonor of her husband.

The papers state that the capture of the Duke by the Vanderbiltian millions will result in bringing the bride's parents together again—that they will re-marry. It is a consummation devoutly to be wished. They seem to have been made for each other—to harmonize in tastes and habits almost as well as did old John Churchill and Sara Jennings. In view of the aphorism that "like takes to like," I cannot imagine how they came to drift apart. If Mrs. Vanderbilt is looking for a rake, Willie should please her to perfection. If he admires dizzy females, she's the girl for his gold. If Willie loves the rapid in crinoline he should fairly worship his *ci-devant* wife. Let them forgive and forget and enjoy to the utmost the beatitude of having a sure-enough Duke for a son-in-law — of referring to their daughter in the presence of those stuck up Goulds as "the Duchess." Willie and Alva should spend a few months of each year at Blenheim Palace—a place so noted in the annals of prostitution. Vive la Van Der Bilt! Vive la Marlborough! The representative family of American parvenues and that of European pimps in holy alliance were a combination at which the majestic world may well stand agaze.

BRANN VS. SLATTERY

The author gained fast and far renown by his slashing denunciation of lecturer Joseph Slattery, self-styled ex-priest, who spoke at Waco on the subject of the Catholic Church and its alleged abuses. Without doubt, Brann's unexpected fusillade reduced Slattery and his group to the realm of the ridiculous.

[Ex-Priest Joseph Slattery, in his lectures at Waco, Texas, in the interests of the A. P. A., having bitterly denounced the Iconoclast, Mr. Brann replied to him as follows:]

Fellow Americans: The Iconoclast does not please ex-Priest Slattery, "Baptist minister in good standing," and I am not surprised. Its mission, as its name implies, is to expose Frauds and abolish Fakes, to make unrelenting war upon Humbugs and Hypocrites; hence it is not remarkable that Slattery should regard its existence as a personal affront. It is ever the galled jade that winces; or, to borrow from the elegant pulpit vernacular of the Rev. Sam Jones, "it's the hit dog that yelps."

Slattery would have you believe that I'm a rank atheist who's trying to rip religion up by the roots and bang it across a barbed wire fence in close companionship with the hides of Protestant preachers. This charge has been hurled at me by various sectarian papers and malicious ministers; but not one iota of evidence has ever been submitted. It is simply a bald assertion born of sanctified malice, a brazen libel, similar to that which charges the Pope with trying to subvert the American government. I defy Slattery and all that unclean brood of moral vultures, assassins of character and thieves of reputation which trail in his wake and applaud his infamies, to produce one line I ever wrote, or quote one sentence I ever uttered disrespectful of *any* religion, Pagan, Protestant or Catholic. If in the wilds of Central Africa I should find a man bowing down to a dried toad, a stuffed snake or a Slattery, I'd remove my hat as a tribute of respect, not to his judgment, but to his honesty. I have no word of condemnation for any religious faith, however fatuous it may appear to me, that has comforted the dying or consoled the living—that has cast one gleam of supernal sunshine into the dark vale where grope, each beneath his burthen of sorrow, the sons of men. I am not warring upon religious faith, but on falsehood; not upon Christ, but on those who disgrace his cause—who mistake bile for benevolence, gall for godliness and chronic laziness for "a call to preach."

Nor have I taken the Pope of Rome under my apostolic protection. The Popes managed to exist for a great many years before I was born, and, despite the assaults of Slattery, will doubtless continue in business at the old stand for several years to come. I was raised a Protestant, and—thank God!—I'm no apostate. I learned Protestantism at my mother's knee, and from my father's pulpit; but I did not learn there that the Church of Rome is the "Scarlet Woman," nuns unclean creatures and priests the sworn enemies of my country. I learned that but for the Church of Rome the "glad tidings of great joy," which Christ brought to a dying world, would have been irredeemably lost in that dismal intellectual night known as the Dark Ages. I was taught that for centuries the Church of Rome was the repository, not only of the Christian faith, but of civilization itself. I was taught that the Catholic is the mother of the Protestant church, and that no matter how unworthy a parent may be, a child should not become the herald of its mother's shame.

And while being taught my duty as a Protestant, my education as an American citizen was not neglected. I was taught that this was a land of religious liberty, where every man is privileged to worship God in his own way, or ignore him altogether; that it was my duty to insist upon this right, both for myself and for my fellows.

That is why I am the uncompromising enemy of the A. P. A.

Any attempt to debar an American citizen from the honors and emoluments of a public office because of his religious faith, is a flagrant violation of a fundamental principle of this Republic. And no patriot; no man in whose veins there pulses one drop of the blood of the Conscript Fathers, or who would recognize the Goddess of Liberty if he met her in the road; no man imbued with the tolerant spirit of the Lord Jesus Christ will aid or abet such an un-Christian and un-American movement. The A. P. A. is the bastard spawn of Ignorance and Intolerance, was conceived in sin and brought forth in iniquity.

There may be some honest men connected with the movement; but if honest they should get their heads trepanned to give their brains room to grow. They are as unable as a mule-eared rabbit to comprehend either the broad principles upon which this government is grounded, or its political and religious history. No man—not even Judas Iscariot Slattery—is to blame for his ignorance; so we should humbly pray, Father forgive them, they know not what they do. Nor is the Church of Rome responsible for the shameless apostate's lack of information. It did all that it could to transform him from an ignorant little beggar into an educated gentleman—but even the Pope cannot make a silk purse of a sow's ear. It is no fault of the Church of Rome that he's densely ignorant of the very textbook truths of history; that he knows less than nothing of that Reformation of which he talks so glibly; that he is unable to comprehend the genius of the government upon which he has conferred his more or less valuable citizenship. The fault, if fault it be, lies with the Almighty, who gave him a bad heart and a worse head.

* * *

American Protective Association, eh? That signifies that Uncle Sam is in need of protection. I had hitherto supposed that the gentleman in the highwater pants and star-bespangled cutaway was able to protect himself; but it now appears that unless he crawls under the aegis of the redoubtable Slattery he is—to again borrow from the most popular of all Protestant divines—"a gone sucker." Think of placing Uncle Sam under the protection of a man who is an apostate in religion and a renegade in politics—of an Irishman who apostrophizes the British flag! Think of that kind of a bird presuming to tell the grandsons of Revolutionary soldiers their duties as American citizens.

Slattery assures us that we need protection from the Pope. There was a time when the proudest monarchs of Europe trembled at the Papal nod; but gradually the Pope has been shorn of temporal power, confined ever more to the realm of spiritual, until today he exerts about as little influence on the political destiny of this world as does Dr. Cranfill with his little Prohibition craze. But Slattery will have it that the Pope is gradually undermining American institutions—leads us to infer that, sooner or later, he'll blow our blessed constitution at the moon and scatter fragments of the Goddess of Liberty from Dan to Beersheba, from Cape Cod to Kalamazoo. The Pope, it appears, is a veritable Guy Faux, who is tunnelling beneath our national capitol with a keg of giant powder in one hand and a box of lucifer matches in the other. What's the evidence? Why, out in San Francisco, so Slattery says—but as Slattery's been convicted of lying it were well to call for papers—a Catholic school board was elected and employed only Catholic teachers. The same awful thing happened in Detroit—if Slattery's telling the truth, which is doubtful in the extreme. Then what? With a pride worthy of a more American act, this illogical idiot informs us that "when the Protestants captured the school boards of those cities they discharged every one of the Catholic teachers and put only good Protestants on guard." And at that Baptist brethren—with water on the brain—who boast of Roger Williams, cheered so loudly as to be in danger of lockjaw. In the exuberant imagination of Slattery and his dupes there appears to be a wonderful difference between tweedledum and tweedledee. It doesn't seem to have occurred to them that what is sauce for the Protestant goose should be sauce for the Catholic gander. They damn the Catholics for doing the very thing for which they commend the Protestant. That's the logic of the A. P. A.—the Aggregation of Pusillanimous Asses. In my humble opinion both were engaged in very small business. The only difference in the offenders that I can see is that while the Catholics are saying nothing, the Protestants are loudly boasting of religious liberty. The circumstance is a sharp reminder that if we are to preserve a government of the people, for the people and by the people, we've got to keep religion of *all* kinds out of our politics, just as the framers of the federal constitution intended that we should do. Mixing religion and politics is like mixing whiskey and water—it spoils both.

Slattery would have you believe that our Catholic citizens are simply emissaries of the Pope, to whom they owe allegiance both spiritual and temporal, and that they will, at the first opportunity, subvert American institutions and make this Nation simply a satrapy of the Vatican.

The American Catholic takes his theology from Rome; he takes his politics from the ecumenical council of his party—from the national convention of that partisan organization to which he may chance to belong.

That there can be no "Catholic conspiracy" against the free institutions of this country must be evident to every man of common sense from the simple fact that Catholics are divided among all the political parties—are continually voting against each other. Now I appeal to your judgment—lay aside your religious prejudices for the moment and look at the matter from a non-partisan, non-sectarian standpoint: If our Catholic fellow citizens be under the thumb of the Pope politically, as the apostate now evangelizing for the A. P. A. would have us believe; and if the Pope desires to make himself temporal ruler of this land, or in any manner direct its affairs, would they not be found voting as a unit—a mighty political machine—instead of being as badly divided on secular questions as the Baptists themselves? San Antonio is a Catholic stronghold, yet a prominent Roman Catholic was overwhelmingly defeated in the last mayoralty election. And I could cite you hundreds of instances where Catholics have voted against men of their own religious faith and elected Protestants or infidels.

Again: If the Pope is plotting against America; and if all manner of crime be considered a virtue when committed by Catholics in furtherance of his ends, as Slattery would have you believe, then it were well to keep a sharp eye on apostate priests. How are we to know that they are not emissaries of the Vatican, commissioned to stir the Protestants up to persecute their brethren in Christ and thereby solidify the Catholic vote? No one, not even Slattery, has accused the Pope of being a fool; and certain it is that the A. P. A. movement, if persisted in, will have the effect of driving the Catholics of this country to political unity in self-defense. Persecution, political ostracism for religious opinion's sake, will infallibly bring about those very conditions which Slattery, Hicks, et al. declare that the Pope desires. The communicants of the Church of Rome will no longer vote as Democrats or Republicans, but as Catholics—and then? With unlimited wealth, and such a political machine at the command of a man so ambitious and unscrupulous as we are asked to believe the Pope to be, the capture of the federal government and the political domination of this country were as easy as lying! The Protestants, divided into a hundred warring factions, many of them farther apart theologically than Episcopalianism and Catholicism, could offer no resistance to such a political machine, and they would receive but cold comfort from the liberal element, which has suffered so long from their petty persecutions.

And I tell you Protestants right here, that if it be the intention of the Church of Rome to transform this government into a theocracy by fair means or foul, then the Pope is the real founder of the A. P. A. and Slattery's a Papal spy.

* * *

According to the story of this self-constituted protector of the American government, he studied Roman Catholic theology for years, then officiated as a priest for eight more before discovering anything immoral in the teachings of the Mother Church, when it suddenly occurred to him that it was but a tissue of falsehoods, a veritable cesspool of rottenness. His transformation appears to have been almost as sudden as that of Saul of Tarsus—or that of Judas Iscariot. I have no objection to his leaving the Catholic priesthood—his bishop stopped his pay. Like the servant maid caught pilfering, he "gave notice, with the missus a-pintin' at the door." If Slattery believes that the Protestant Through Line runs more comfortable cars to the great hereafter, he's welcome to take his ticket on that route; but I would have thought better of him had he made the change quietly and refrained from assaulting with the vindictiveness of a renegade that church to which he owes his education, such as it is; had he treated the religion of his mother with decency if not with respect.

I thought I had met all manner of men; men hardened in crime—men destitute of even a semblance of shame; but never before did I behold one with the hardihood to stand up before American women and boast that he had incurred a mother's curse. When a man falls so low in the scale of human degradation that his own mother disowns him it were well to watch him. When a creature asks strangers to accept him because his relatives have rejected him; when, for the sake of gain, he snaps like a mangy fice at the hand that once fed him, and stings like a poisonous adder the bosom that once nurtured him; when, to promote his personal ends, he will use his best endeavors to exterminate religious liberty and precipitate a bloody sectarian war, I tell you he was not born a man but begotten a beast.

From the very foundation of this government the Catholics have been its firm defenders. Their wisdom and eloquence have adorned its councils from the signing of the Declaration of American Independence to this good day, and its every battlefield, from Lexington to the Custer massacre, has been wet with Catholic blood. Nine Roman Catholics signed the Declaration of Independence, and the Roman Catholics of New York contributed so liberally of their blood and treasure to the cause of the new-born Nation that Washington wrote them a letter praising their patriotism. Several Roman Catholics helped frame the Federal Constitution, and the interpretation of that wonderful instrument by a Roman Catholic chief justice today constitutes the fundamental law of the land. Yet Slattery and that ridiculous organization of which he boasts himself a member, would have you believe that the American Catholics would, at a nod from the Pope, ruthlessly trample under foot that flag in whose defense they pledged their lives, their fortunes and their sacred honor—that they would wreck without remorse and ruin without regret that Nation they helped place on the map of the world. How do you old Confederates, who followed Pat Cleburne, relish having this blatant tramp defame your dead commander? Can you believe, on the unsupported testimony of this mendacious mountebank, that Father Ryan's tribute to the Stars-and-Bars was rank hypocrisy—that the poet-priest was the political tool of a foreign power? Sherman died a Catholic. Fighting Phil Sheridan was a Catholic. Old Pap Thomas, "the Rock of Chickamauga," was a Catholic. The "Bloody Sixty-ninth" New York was a Catholic regiment, and its heroism at the Battle of Bull Run forms one of the brightest pages in the military history of this nation. Strange it never occurred to those demoralized Protestant regiments which took refuge behind the bayonets of the Sixty-ninth that they were throwing the Vatican between themselves and the Confederate forces!

Slattery assures us that the number of Irish Catholics on the police force of our great cities is evidence that the Church of Rome is on mischief bent. I am not surprised that an Irish Catholic with a club in his hand should prove rather alarming to Bro. Slattery. But, although he says, "meet a policeman and you'll see the map of Ireland in his face," those same policemen have several times saved his worthless bacon. When he was mobbed in St. Louis for defaming Catholic nuns, the police formed a cordon around his infamous carcass and saved him from a well-merited trouncing at the hands of the slandered women's relatives. Probably the police did not relish the job overmuch, but they had sworn to uphold the laws, and although Slattery insists that a Catholic oath amounts to nothing, they risked their lives in his defense.

We have many nationalities in this country, and each of them, as every observant man well knows, manifests a predilection for some special occupation. Thus the Jews take to trade, the Germans to agriculture, the Norwegians to lumbering, the French to catering and the Irish to politics. Make a Freewill Baptist or a Buddhist of an Irishman and you do not change his nature—he'll turn up at the next political convention just the same. And the man who's too good to take a hand in practical politics; who's too nice to mingle with the horny-handed at the ward primaries; who's too busy to act as delegate to the convention—who deliberately neglects his duty as an American citizen—finds that Pat's activity has been rewarded with a place on the police force, and blames it all on the Pope.

* * *

It is not my province to defend Roman Catholic theology—I suppose that Slattery said all that could be urged in its behalf before the apostatized. Perhaps the Catholics really believe the Pope infallible; and if they do, it is certainly no worse than for certain Waco Protestants to believe that Slattery's infallible. I noticed that at his lecture last week they cheered every charge he preferred against either the Pope or the "Apostle," and that without asking for an iota of evidence. When I arose at the stag party with which he wound up the intellectual debauch, and questioned his infallibility, the good brethren cried, "Throw him out!" Why did they so unless they believed that to question the supernal wisdom and immaculate truth of aught a Baptist minister might say, were sacrilege—a sin against the Holy Ghost?

Here was I, their fellow citizen of Waco. I had done them no harm; yet when a strolling vagabond, wearing God's livery, and whose forte is the defamation of women, made a statement, which if true, would forever disgrace me in the eyes of the world; when he preferred this charge against me within two blocks of where my babies lay sleeping, they wanted to mob me for branding him then and there as an infamous liar and a cowardly blackguard.

Mark you, I'm no tramp in America. This is the house of my fathers. They helped hew it out of the Virginia wilderness. They helped put Old Glory in the heavens, and to keep it there for more than a hundred years; still it appears that I have no rights in this country which a foreigner with the smell of the steerage still upon him is bound to respect, if he chances to be a Baptist preacher.

Talk to me about the Church of Rome muzzling free speech when the A. P. A. would mob an American citizen for defending his character from the infamous falsehoods of a foreign tramp! "Throw him out!" Why throw him out? I'll tell you: The sanctified buzzards had gone there with appetites sharpened for a mess of carrion, and they were afraid I'd kill their cook. "Throw him out!" But I noticed that those who were splitting their faces as wide as Billy Kersands' were glued to their seats. They wanted somebody else to throw him out. They were anxious to see a gang of three or four hundred sanctified hoodlums trample upon me, but there was not one among the self-constituted protectors of this mighty American Nation with sufficient "sand" to lead the mob. If there were no better Americans than those trailing in the wake of the Rev. Joseph Slattery, like buzzards following a bad smell, I'd take a cornstalk, clean out the whole shooting-match and stock the country with niggers and yaller dogs. If such cattle were sired by Satan, dammed by Sycorax and born in hell they would dishonor their parents and disgrace their country.

Slattery insists that Catholics believe thus-and-so, and that no man with such a faith concealed about his person can be a good American citizen. I don't know about that; but I do know that if the Catholic act in strict accordance with their religious creed they are the only people in this country that do so. I've learned that you can't judge a man by his catechism. Slattery assures us that he has discarded the Pope and taken Christ for his immediate guide. The latter commands his followers to pray for those who despitefully use them; but if Slattery did any praying for the "Apostle" during his sojourn in this city he managed to keep that fact a profound secret. Christ enjoins patience and humility. He tells his followers to turn the other cheek to the smiter; yet Slattery assured the ladies Wednesday night that he was "a great believer in muscular Christianity." Then he placed his 250 pounds of stall-fed beef in fighting attitude and declared he'd "like to have his enemies come at him one at a time"—to be prayed for, I presume. If Christ taught "muscular Christianity" I have inadvertently overlooked a bet. Christ commands us to love our enemies, but doesn't suggest that we should manifest our affection by lying about 'em. He rebuked those who tattled about a common courtesan, yet Slattery defamed decent women. No, you can't judge a man by his creed. If the allegiance of the Catholics to the Pope is of the same character as that of Slattery to the Lord Jesus Christ, Uncle Sam need not lie awake o' nights to worry about "Papal plots."

Had Slattery been truly a Christian, instead of blackguarding me when protected by the presence of ladies, he would have put up a fervent prayer for my immediate conversion to the Baptist faith. But his milk of human kindness had soured—he was short on Christian charity and long on gall.

"Faith, hope and charity," says St. Paul; "and the greatest of these is charity." And he might have added that it's also the scarcest. Perhaps that's what makes it so valuable—the supply is never equal to the demand.

Speaking of charity reminds me of my experience with the Protestant preachers of San Antonio, some of whom, I understand, are aiding and abetting this A. P. A. movement, "designed to preserve the priceless liberty of free speech." While editor of the morning paper of that city I was in the habit of writing a short sermon for the Sunday edition, for the benefit of those who could not go to church, I supposed that the ministers would sanction my clerical efforts, but they didn't. They wanted no assistance in saving souls, considered that they should be accorded a monopoly in that line and were entitled to all the emoluments. They proceeded to thunder at me from the pulpit, and sometimes three or four perspiring pulpiteers were pounding away at me at the same time—and incidentally making me very popular. I dropped into a swell church one Sunday morning to get a little grace—a building that cost up in the six figures while people were living in $4 jackals and subsisting on 50 cents a week within sound of its bells—and the minister was holding a copy of the *Express* aloft in one hand and a Bible in the other and demanding of his congregation: "Which will you take—Brann or God?" Well, they seemed to think that if they couldn't have both they'd best take God, tho' some of the sinners on the back seats were a trifle subsequent in making up their minds.

I kept hammering away—preaching to my little congregation of fifteen or twenty thousand readers every Sunday, as I now do to ten times that many a month—until finally the Ministerial Association met, perorated, whereased, resoluted and wound up by practically demanding of the proprietor of the *Express* that I be either muzzled or fired. And all this time the Catholic priests said never a word—and San Antonio is a Catholic city. But the Baptist ministers were running a sneaking boycott! Yet the Church of Rome is the boa-constrictor that's trying to throttle the American right of free speech!

The Y.M.C.A. invited me to lecture on Humbugs, and that scared the Ministerial Association nearly to death. They thought I was after 'em now sure, so they went to the officials of the Y.M.C.A. and made them cancel the date. And the only Protestant minister in the entire city who did not join in this attempt to throttle free speech was an Episcopalian—and the Episcopalians are not Protestants to hurt. Yet when these ministers, who are now so fearful that the Church of Rome will muzzle somebody, found that they couldn't drive me out of town; that they couldn't take the bread from the mouths of my babes because I had dared utter my honest thoughts like a freeman; that I was to continue to edit the *Express* so long as I liked, they came fawning about me like a lot of spaniels afraid of the lash! But not one of them ever tried to convert me. Not one of them ever tried, by kindly argument, to convince me that I was wrong. Not one of them ever invited me to church—or prayed for me, so far as I could learn. Perhaps they thought I was past redemption.

* * *

Slattery cautions you not to send your children to convent schools, declaring that he "never yet saw a nun who was an educated woman." That statement, standing alone, ought to convince every one blessed with a thinking apparatus that Slattery's a fraud. Some of the best educated women in this world have entered convents. Women upon whose tuition fortunes have been expended are now making convent schools deservedly popular with the intelligent people.

He says ignorance is the correlative of Catholicism, and points to Spain as proof of this startling assertion. There was a time when Spain stood in the very forefront of civilization, in the van of human progress, the arbiter of the world's political destiny,—and Spain was even more Catholic then than it is today. Nations and civilizations have their youth, their lusty manhood and their decay, and it were idle to attribute the decline of Spain to Catholicism as the decadence of Greece to Paganism. The Catholic Church found Spain a nation of barbarians and brought it up to that standard of civilization where a Spanish monarch could understand the mighty plans of Columbus. It was her Catholic Majesty, Queen Isabella, who took from her imperial bosom the jewels with which to buy a world—who exchanged the pearls of the Orient for the star of Empire. The Catholic Church found England a nation of barbarians and brought it up, step by step, until Catholic barons wrung from King John at Runnymede the Great Charter—the mother of the American Constitution. It found Ireland a nation of savages and did for it what the mighty power of the Caesars could not—brought it within the pale of civilization. But for the Roman Catholic Church Slattery might be wearing a breech clout, digging roots with his fingernails and gorging himself with raw meat in Ireland today instead of insulting the intelligence of American audiences and wringing money from fanatics and fools by warring upon the political institutions of their fathers.

* * *

Slattery was horrified to learn that some of the nuns were inclined to talk about each other. I sincerely trust that he will find none of the Baptist sisters addicted to the same bad habit.

From what I could gather of his discourse,—before I was "put out"—and from the report of his alleged wife's lectures, I infer that this delectable twain impeach the virtue of the Roman Catholic sisterhoods. Malice, like death, loves a shining mark, and there is no hate so venomous as that of the apostate. But before giving credence to such tales, let me ask you: Why should a woman exchange the brilliant parlor for a gloomy cell in which to play the hypocrite? Why should a cultured woman of gentle birth deliberately forego the joys of wife and motherhood, the social triumph and the freedom of the world and condemn herself to a life of labor, a dreary round of drudgery, if her heart's impure? For shame!

Who is it that visits the slums of our great cities ministering to the afflicted, comforting the dying, reclaiming the fallen? When pestilence sweeps over the land and mothers desert their babes and husbands their wives, who is it that presses the cup of cold water to the feverish lip and closes the staring eyes of the deserted dead? Who was it that went upon the Southern battlefields to minister to the wounded soldiers, followed them to the hospitals and tenderly nursed them back to life? The Roman Catholic sisterhoods, God bless them!

One of those angels of mercy can walk unattended and unharmed thro' our "Reservation" at midnight. She can visit with impunity the most degraded dive in the White-chapel district. At her coming the ribald song is stilled and the oath dies on the lips of the loafer. Fallen creatures reverently touch the hem of her garments, and men steeped in crime to the very lips involuntarily remove their hats as a tribute to noble womanhood. The very atmosphere seems to grow sweet with her coming and the howl of hell's demons to grow silent. None so low in the barrel-house, the gambling hell or the brothel as to breathe a word against her good name; but when we turn to the Baptist pulpit there we find an inhuman monster clad in God's livery, saying, "Unclean, unclean!" God help a religious denomination that will countenance such an infamous cur!

As a working journalist I have visited all manner of places. I have written up the foulest dives that exist on this continent, and have seen Sisters of Charity enter them unattended. Had one of the inmates dared insult them he would have been torn to pieces. And I have sat in the opera house of this city—boasting itself a center of culture—and heard a so-called man of God speak flippantly of the Catholic sisterhoods, and professing Christians applaud him to the echo.

Merciful God! if heaven is filled with such Christians, send me to hell, with those whose sins are inhuman! Better everlasting life in a lake of fire than enforced companionship in Paradise for one hour with the foul harpies that groaned "awmen" to Slattery's infamous utterances. God of Israel! to think that those unmanly scabs, those psalm-singing vultures are Americans and our political brethren!

* * *

I know little about the private lives of the Catholic priesthood; but this I do know: They were the first to plant the standard of Christian faith in the New World. They were the first to teach the savages something of the blessings of civilization. I do know that those of them who were once Protestants are not making a specialty of defaming the faith of their fathers. I do know that neither hardship nor danger can abate their holy zeal and that hundreds of them have freely given their lives in the service of the Lord. And why should a man devote his body to God and his soul to the devil? I do know that one of them has given us the grandest example of human sacrifice for others' sake that this great world affords. Even Christ prayed in the Garden of Gethsemane, "If it be possible, let this cup pass from me;" but Father Damien pressed a cup even more bitter to his own lips and drained it to the dregs—died for the sake of suffering mortals a death to which the cross were mercy.

The Protestants admit that they are responsible for the inoculation of the simple Sandwich Islanders with the leprosy; yet when those who fell victims to the foul disease were segregated, made prisoners upon a small island in the mid-Pacific, not a Protestant preacher in all the earth could be found to minister to them . The Lord had "called" 'em all into his vineyard, but it appears that he didn't call a blessed one of them to that leper colony where people were rotting alive, with none to point them to that life beyond the grave where all the sins and corruptions of the flesh are purged away and the redeemed stand in robes of radiant white at the right hand of God. I blame no man for declining the sacrifice. To set foot upon that accursed spot was to be declared unclean and there confined until death released you—death by leprosy, the most appalling disease in all the dreadful catalogue of human ills, the most dreaded arrow in the quiver of the grim Destroyer. Yet Father Damien, a young Roman Catholic priest, left home and country and all that life holds dear, and went deliberately forth to die for afflicted barbarians. There he reared an humble temple with his own hands to the God of his fathers, there, thro' long years of confinement, he ministered to the temporal and spiritual wants of the afflicted; there he died, as he knew he must die, with his fingers falling from his hands, his flesh from his bones, a sight to appall the very imps of hell. No wonder the Protestant ministers held aloof. Merciful God. I'd rather be crucified!

We are all brave men when the war-drum throbs and the trumpet calls us to do battle beneath the eyes of the world,—when, touching elbows with our fellows and clad in all the glorious pomp and circumstance of war we seek the bubble of fame e'en at the cannon's mouth. When the music of the battery breeds murder in the blood, the electric order goes ringing down the line, is answered by the thrilling cheer, the veriest coward drives the spur deep into the foaming flank and plunges, like a thunderbolt, into the gaping jaws of death, into the mouth of hell; but when a man was wanted to go forth alone, without blare of trumpet or drum, and become a life-prisoner in a leper colony, but one in all the world could be found equal to that supreme test of personal heroism, and that man was a Roman Catholic priest. And what was his reward? Hear what Thos. Sherman, a good Protestant, says in the New York *Post:*

"Before the missionaries gained control of the islands leprosy was unknown. But with the introduction of strange races, leprosy established itself and rapidly increased. An entire island was properly devoted to the lepers. No Protestant missionary would venture among them. For this I do not blame them, as, no doubt, I should not have had the courage to go myself. But a noble Catholic priest consecrated his life to the service of the lepers, lived among them, baptized them, educated them, and brought some light and happiness into their wretched lives. Stung by the contrast of his example, the one remaining missionary, a recognized and paid agent of the American Board, spread broadcast the vilest slanders against Father Damien."

So it appears that the world is blessed with two Slatterys.

There are three kinds of liars at large in the land: The harmless Munchausen who romances for amusement, and whose falsehoods do no harm; the Machiavellian liar, whose mendacity bears the stamp of original genius, and the stupid prevaricator, who rechews the fetid vomit of other villains simply because he lacks a fecund brain to breed falsehoods to which he may play the father. And Slattery's a rank specimen of the latter class. When he attempts to branch out for himself he invariably comes to grief. After giving a dreadful account of how Catholics persecute those who renounce the faith, declaring that they were a disgrace to the church while within its pale, he produced a certificate from a Philadelphia minister to the effect that he—the Philadelphian—had visited Slattery's old parish in Ireland and the Catholics there declared that he was a good and faithful priest! What Slattery seems to lack to become a first-class fraud is continuity of thought. He lies fluently, even entertainingly, but not consistently.

The apostate priest would have the various Protestant denominations throw down the bars that separate them and mark off their theological bailiwicks "with little beds of flowers." The idea is a good one—and I can but wonder where Slattery stole it. Still I can see no cogent reason for getting all the children together in happy union and leaving their good old mother out in the cold.

Throw down all the bars, and let every division of the Great Army of God, whether wearing the uniform of Buddhist or Baptist, Catholic or Campbellite, Methodist or Mohammedan, move forward, with Faith its sword, Hope its ensign and Charity its shield. Cease this foolish internecine strife, at which angels weep, swing into line as sworn allies and, at the command of the Great Captain, advance your standards on the camp of the common foe. Wage war, not upon each other, but on Poverty, Ignorance and Crime, hells great triumvirate, until this beautiful world's redeemed are bound in very truth,

"With gold chains about the feet of God."

ISRAEL AS IT IS

Again playing the advocate in an unexpected quarter, Brann makes a scholarly and telling defense for Judaism and the Jew.

There was a time when to have sprung from Judah's consecrated loins was better than to be born a king; when the embattled hosts of Israel made the world tremble before their martial might, and men turned for knowledge to Zion's holy hill as the helianthus turns its face to the rising sun.

When our ancestors were but brutal barbarians, clad in skins stripped with sharp stones from beasts scarcely less ferocious; dwelling in caves and subsisting on roots and raw meat; with no aspirations above the crudest creature comforts, no conception of immortality, no dream of man's high destiny, Solomon was making silver as the stones in the streets of Jerusalem; the Jews were worshipping the "Lord of Hosts," framing those laws which are today the basic principle of civilization, quelling semi-barbarous people with the sword, computing the procession of the planets and weaving into the woof of human history those imperishable gems of poesy and philosophy which the world's wisest say transcend the genius of mortal man and must, perforce, be the gracious gift of God.

Yet for twenty centuries we have regarded the Jew with suspicion, treated him as if he were of an inferior race; as though in his bosom beat the heart of an inhuman harpy, in his veins coursed the accursed blood of the wolf. For twenty centuries the Jew has suffered "the oppressor's wrong, the proud man's contumely"—has been the target at which the finger of scorn was ever pointed; the buffet of dissolute princes and purse-proud potentates; the undeserving victim of the blind wrath of the proletarian rabble; the mark at which sectarian hate and unreasoning bigotry have levelled their most vindictive shafts; despoiled, outraged, beaten with many stripes; expatriated, driven hither and thither, finding no rest for his weary feet in a world which his wisdom has done so much to humanize, to which he has given happiness here and hope hereafter.

Is it possible that the Jew, who is of the blood and bone of the patriarchs and prophets, of Moses the Medianite, and those warlike Maccabees before whom the fierce Syrian soldiery fled terror-stricken from Judea's hills, is a creature fit only for our contumely, a dog to be spurned by "Christian" feet? That the children of men who, cooped up in one quarter of their beloved city and dying of starvation, defended their holy temple against Titus the Terrible and the intrepid sons of all-conquering Rome until the sacred pile was dripping with blood and ablaze with the legionary's brand, but merit the sneers of a people whose ancestors a few generations ago were plowing the Northern seas as pirates in quest of plunder, or participating in the bloody and brutal rites of the Druidical superstition?

To deny that there is a widespread antipathy to the Jew were as fatuous as to deny the existence of the sun. In most parts of the United States this antipathy is latent; but in Europe it not only manifests itself in legislation and social ethics, but frequently bursts forth in deeds of desperate violence and inhumanity on the part of the people. Even while I write, in "Christian" Russia the Jews are being despoiled and outraged—their homes given to the flames, their savings to the plunderer, their daughters to the ravisher, their throats to the knife! And the rest of the so-called Christian world mildly protests; intimates that, perhaps, after all, the Jew has a soul, at least flesh and bone, and may suffer somewhat.

While the Tsar's brutal soldiery—aided by the volunteer efforts of the Russian peasantry and such other people as consider the killing of a creditor the easiest way to discharge an honest debt—are hurrying the Jews across the frontiers, the civilized world is firing whereases, resolutions, remonstrances signed by aldermen and fledgling D. D.'s, silly tirades by alleged able editors and other trifling nonsense and cheap balderdash at his "Most Christian Majesty;" then, convinced that it has done its duty, it goes home to dinner—perhaps with a half defined feeling that nobody has any business to be a Jew! Were the people of any other race subjected to such barbarous brutality, the Christian world, so-called, would demand that it cease instantly, and demand it sword in hand.

The cause of this prejudice against the Jew, which appears to be bred in the very bone of "Christian" people of Indo-European blood, it were indeed difficult to determine. Scarcely a count in the formidable indictment which has hung over him for a hundred generations like a veritable sword of Damocles, will stand analysis. It is charged that the Jew will not intermarry with other races. In God's name, cannot a man choose a wife to suit himself without having a whole majestic universe snarling at his heels? If the dark-eyed daughters of Judah prefer their kinsmen to those who from time immemorial have persecuted them, cannot a professedly chivalrous world leave them free to choose? Is it at all strange that a people whose blood for two thousand years has been kept free from taint, should decline to pour it into that great red tide which has greedily absorbed every clean and unclean thing with which it has come in contact, whether Goth or Moor, British barbarian or American red Indian, and is now blending slowly but surely with the Ethiop and Australian Bushman?

But while the incongruous and ofttimes unclean mixture of races in Europe, and especially in America, where the great-grandsons of Charlemagne's paladins wed the great-granddaughters of expatriated sneak thieves and lousy Indian squaws —where the blood of the Capulets mingles with that of the Cades—is of itself sufficient to give pause to those who trace their lineage through God-fearing men and chaste women back to the days of David, it is not the only nor the chief cause why the Jews maintain that solidarity which is at once the wonder of the world and the burthen of its never-ceasing jeremiad. Their religion tends to make the Jews chary of intermarriage with non-conformists; but the great determining cause of their exclusiveness is the social and political ostracism to which they have for so many centuries been generally subjected by the "enlightened," "progressive," "Christian" nations of Europe, and which occasionally shows its ugly front, like Discord at Peleus' nuptial rites, in free America, where anything that can dodge the gallows or the jail for one and twenty years is called a sovereign,—where we buy with our millions the bastard spawn of kings' courtesans as husbands for our daughters!

The Jew was driven into trade and money-changing by the edicts of Christian potentates forbidding him to acquire title to land. In his own country before the diaspora his chief occupation was agriculture, and the law of his religion did not permit him to lend at interest for the relief of distress. Money is power, even in the hands of the Jew, and it is small wonder that when he found it his only friend in a world of fanatical foes—the only weapon with which he could hope to win his way—in sheer self-defense he diligently sought to acquire all of it possible. Money to the Jews has ever meant much more than creature comforts; it has meant sword and shield, bulwark and bastion—the magic wand that metamorphoses the Medusa-face of sectarian hate into that of the oily and unctuous hypocrite.

It is small wonder that in money matters the Jew has become preternaturally keen; small wonder that in dealing with his enemies, actual or potential, he should prove an exacting creditor—should acquire an unenviable reputation among his hereditary critics for sordidness and "sharp practice." But the avarice, so-called, of the Jew, is the result, not the cause of centuries of political and social ostracism. To abuse the Jew for "getting gain" were like throwing a man into a tempestuous sea and cursing him for grasping desperately at whatever may promise preservation. Numerically too weak to force recognition of his right with the naked sword, the Jew forges his weapon of fine gold and with it makes the proudest of Christian potentates pay him homage with their lips while they curse him in their hearts.

So far from being a stony-hearted, avaricious people, as popularly supposed, the Jews are naturally the most sympathetic and generous in the world. Who ever heard of a Jew begging bread, going to the alms-house or suffering for creature comforts, while other members of his race—even though strangers—knowing of his necessities, had a crust to share or a dollar to divide? And yet we "Christians," who prate of our liberality and pose before the world as paragons of philanthropy, ofttimes allow our old mothers to go "on the county" while we go on a champagne "jag;" permit our brothers to eat the bitter bread of a stranger's contemptuous charity, while we parade as public-spirited citizens! Very remarkable is it that while our relatives are usually the last in the world we desire to embark in business with, the Jew prefers his near kinsman to all others. We know our brethren—know that they will rob and betray, "bullyrag" and beat at every opportunity. The Jew knows his brethren and trusts his fortune to their hands without a tremor!

Avaricious? Miserly? Little-souled? Mean? Thou fool! The Jew is the most liberal money-spender in the world. He calls for the best of everything and pays for it like a prince! Did you ever hear that a Jew miser starved to death in the midst of his millions? That one of the race of Judah ever perished for lack of medical attendance which he was too penurious to pay for? Yet such things are of almost daily occurrence in this Christian land! But the victim of the unholy lust for gain is never, no, never, a Jew. He may hide his heart in his money-bags, but never follows the example of Pedro Garcia and keeps his soul there also.

In every corner where the Jew has been accorded the political privileges of other people, he has proven himself a public-spirited citizen, and his subscriptions to enterprises to promote the public welfare have been paid promptly and without protest. While the Christian has given his "moral support," the Jew has gone down into his pockets and planked down the wherewithal that "makes the world go round."

Another count in the indictment is that the Jew never really identifies himself with the country in which he resides—never becomes a patriot; that he is eager to enjoy the rights of citizenship while shirking its responsibilities—anxious for the protection of a flag he will not lift a hand to defend. This is, perhaps, the most remarkable of all the multifarious phases in which ingrained prejudice and hereditary hatred has bodied itself forth. Although the Jewish contingent in our eleemosynary institutions and penitentiaries is practically nil, they are largely supported by taxes paid by the Jewish people. True, the Jew is seldom the central figure at party primaries; his voice rarely adds to the discordant din of partisan polemics; he is seldom seen on the stump at crossroads or the beer barrel in bar rooms, telling his fellow citizens what to do to be saved. He rarely makes of himself a moral bankrupt or noisy nuisance trying to capture an office with small salary and large stealage:—but he can generally be counted upon to cast his ballot for the "conservative" candidate and pay his taxes promptly. Furthermore, when he finds that country in danger which treats him a few degrees better than a dog, he can be depended upon to risk his life and fortune in its defense. Compared with percentage of population, the Jewish contingent in the Federal and Confederate forces was very large, and precious few circumcised soldiers were arrested for bounty-jumping, reprimanded for cowardice or court-martialed for desertion. Many Jews rose to military distinction during the Civil War, and the descendants of Miles Standish, Mad Anthony Wayne, Light-Horse Harry Lee and Francis Marion were proud to call them their commanders. Who can forget the services to the South of Judah Benjamin, or the heroic fortitude with which the Jews stood by the failing Confederacy "with their fortunes, their lives and their sacred honor?" But for the financial aid of the Northern Jews when the tide of battle appeared to be turning against the Federal government and the mighty structure seemed tottering to its fall; when the British lion was crouching for a spring, and even France looked askance at the wounded eagle, the mailed hand of the mighty North would have fallen nerveless as that of a frightened child, the stars and bars would float south of the Ohio, and that scourge of God, negro slavery, be fixed on this fair land forever.

Since the Jews became numerous in Europe and America there has been scarce a battlefield not dyed with Israel's consecrated blood; scarcely a military maneuver not paid for from Jewish purses; scarce a throne not gilded by Jewish industry; scarce a printed page upon which, directly or indirectly, they did not set their seal; scarce a poet who did not borrow their musical metaphors; scarce an orator who did not tacitly acknowledge in every sentence that but for the Jews he would have nothing to say.

From the loins of Judah have sprung more intellectual giants than any other race or nation can boast. The roster of those who have added to the world's wisdom, to human happiness, stretches in an unbroken line from the present hour back to the dawn of human history. Did you ever stop to reflect that Spinoza, the prince of philosophers, Mendelssohn, the master of the world of music, and a host of others whom we revere as something almost more than mortal, not to mention the Christ, whom we worship as a God, were all of the race which you profess to despise? The cause of the prejudice against the Jews is multifarious. He is emphatically a child of the Orient—as different from the Occidentals as though native of another planet. The brawny and intensely practical Scotch Highlander and the mild-eyed melancholy lotus-eater could scarce be further apart from an ethnological standpoint than the Jews and the Indo-Germanic people. Race, political and religious differences bred antipathy long before the destruction of the Second Temple. Then as the Jews dispersed over Europe, came the ill-wind of business rivalry, the hatred of the debtor for the creditor class, followed by the fierce fires of religious bigotry that made of mediaeval Europe a hell upon which Caius Caligula might have looked with horror. In those fierce Gehenna-fires were forged the chains that still hold the Christian mind in thrall; in those dark days when intolerance was lord paramount, when superstition was the handmaiden of religion and the Christian cavalier drove into the ground his sword, stained with the blood of non-conforming maidens, and fell upon his knees before the reeking cross that formed the hilt; when with whip and faggot, the thumb-screw and the wheel, fanatics dragged men to the throne of Grace, or drove them to the Devil, the vulpine instinct of the Jew attained, perforce, an abnormal development, distrust of those not of his race and religion became hereditary. He found the world against him, and it is his misfortune, not his fault, that his hand is against the world.

That the spirit of the Jews has not been utterly crushed by twenty centuries of systematic oppression; that they have not withered beneath the terrible baptism of fire, degenerated into contemptible spiritless lazzaroni; that the united world has signally failed to trample them beneath its brutal feet and keep them there; that despite two thousand years of trial and temptation, of calumny, intimidation, of the most brutal outrages recorded in Time's too unhappy annals, the daughters of Judah are today the paragons of purity, as they have ever been of beauty, proclaims to every man with eyes to see and brain to understand, that the Jews are one of the greatest races, one of the grandest peoples that ever appeared upon the earth; that the Lord of Hosts was infinitely wiser than we when He made His covenant with them and swore by His own bright essence increate, that through good and ill, through weal and woe, He would be their God and they should be His people.

"KING CHARLES THE MARTYR"

ANGLOMANIACISM RUN MAD

In this intemperate essay, appearing in April, 1897, Brann displays forcefully his peculiar detestation of England and the Anglican Church.

It is a trifle difficult for an American to discuss in polite language the recent canonization of Charles I by the Episcopalians of this country. One scarce knows whether to laugh at the ridiculous mummery or be angry with the miserable toad-eating unamericanism of the Episcopal prelacy. It is by no means easy to contemplate in a spirit of toleration, the existence in this country of a church that has ever been the pliant tool and obsequious apologist of tyranny. Episcopalianism in America is like the presence of a pebble in the works of a watch. It is a foreign and disturbing element, and could, like polygamy, be prohibited by law without doing violence to our fundamental principle of religious freedom. Neither individuals nor governments should be expected to ignore the law of self-preservation, and to republican institutions Episcopalianism is a perennial fount of poison. It is the fecund mother of Tories, Anglomaniacs and traitors. From the time when this church was born of the lustful bowels of that royal brute, Henry VIII, to this good hour, it has been the uncompromising foe of freedom. True, it has produced a few American patriots—men who were better than the church to which they belonged; but its tendency is no more toward human liberty than that of Anarchism is toward human law. Scratch a title-worshipper, an Anglomaniac or a snob, and you are pretty apt to find an Episcopalian. Had Charles' beatification, canonization or whatever it may be called, been the horse-play of some obscure prelate of A. P. A. proclivities, it would have merited no attention beyond a *lunatico inquirendo;* but such was not the case. It occurred in Philadelphia, with two bishops officiating in full canonicals, while other prominent prelates sent regrets, assuring the mimers that they were "in cordial sympathy with the occasion." We must accept the unveiling of the portrait of "King Charles the Martyr" as expressive of the religious views and political tendencies of American Episcopalians, hence it may be well to inquire: Who was this "King Charles the Martyr," whose life is so solemnly recommended to Americans as worthy their emulation? He was the victim of that very "Reformation" inaugurated by pious King Henry VIII—at once defender of the Catholic faith and chief of schismatics. He was devoured by the legitimate spawn of that illegitimate monster begotten in Henry's bedchamber and known to history as the Church of England. He was a king who persecuted Calvinists because they would not conform to the Cranmer-corrupted rites of Rome, and persecuted Catholics because they would not accept him as their pope. Although Ireland was true to the House of Stuart, and in every great crisis the mainstay of its throne, he was more cruel to Ireland if possible, than was Cromwell. In religion he was a nondescript, in politics he was a petty tyrant and a professional perjurer. What a pity the solemnly blessed portrait of "King Charles the Martyr" was not accompanied by a few descriptive lines from Macaulay, as passport to the association of Saints. Macaulay, be it remembered, detested "Popery," and described the Anglican Church as the crowning glory of Protestantism; hence we may suppose he was lenient as possible to the royal head of the Anglican hierarchy. He says in part:

> We think his sentence describes him with perfect justice as "a tyrant, a murderer, and a public enemy." * * * * They had to deal with a man who made and broke promises with equal facility, a man whose honor had been a hundred times pawned and never redeemed. * * * * The Puritans were imprisoned. They were whipped. Their ears were cut off. Their noses were slit. Their cheeks were branded with red-hot irons.

Yet when these same Puritans, many of whom did so much to make America what it is, brought the author of these hellish outrages to the block, he became a "blessed martyr" in the eyes of the Anglomaniacs whom we permit to fatten beneath freedom's flag! This is the man who trampled beneath his feet the constitutional rights of our fathers; yet before his portrait an audience of fashionable Americans prostrated themselves while Bishops Coleman and Perry prayed the good God to make us all like unto "Thy servant and martyr, Charles." How do the descendants of the Puritans relish having such an insult flung into their faces by the spawn of those Tories who were prating of "divine right" and preaching the doctrine of "non-resistance" while the streets of Boston were slippery with patriotic blood? How do American Catholics relish this apotheosis of the royal master of Laud and Strafford—the kite and vulture who together preyed upon the vitals of Ireland? Of all the monarchs who have swayed the English sceptre, of all the men who have posed as religious hierarchs, "King Charles the Martyr" was perhaps the meanest. He was true neither to friend nor foe. He had "just ability enough to deceive and just religion enough to persecute." He was selfishness personified, ready at any time to give up his favorites to the vengeance of his foes in return for a parliamentary grant of gold. Persecuting Puritans and Catholics impartially, he was unable to determine his own religious convictions. I could never work up much admiration for the English "Gospelers." At this distance they appear to have had a virulent attack of pseudo-religious *mania a potu;* but I have ever been grateful to Cromwell for bringing that sublimation of selfishness, that incarnation of cruelty, "Charles the blessed Martyr," to the block. As a liar he outranked Ananias; in treachery he could give Iscariot instruction; as a hypocrite he was equalled only by Bishop Cranmer, the first primate of Episcopalianism.

When we consider the history of the Church of England—known in America as the Protestant Episcopal Church—we can scarce wonder that its devotees should beatify a brute, that Charles I should be accorded a place in its calendar. Conceived in sin and brought forth in iniquity, it still bears unmistakable impress of its parentage. Begotten between incestuous sheets, it has been nurtured from its birth on the fruits of robbery and the milk of perfidy. Upon its unclean altars tens of thousands of human beings of both sexes and all ages have been freely sacrificed. The best and bravest of England's children have been passed thro' the fire to glut the pitiless maw of this modern Moloch. William Cobbett, himself a communicant of the Anglican Church, confesses in his "History of the Protestant Reformation," that it was "established by gibbets, racks and ripping knives." A cross between perverted Catholicism and fanatical Calvinism, it inherts the virtues of neither while rank with the vices of both. Its father was a wife-butcher, its mother a bawd—and an evil tree cannot bring forth good fruit. Doubtless we have in America many worthy people who are Episcopalians; but they are communicants of that church only because ignorant of its origin. I have neither time nor inclination to write a history of the Church of England—to trace Episcopalianism from its genesis to the enrollment of Charles among its "blessed Martyrs" by alleged Americans; but in view of the Philadelphia episode, a few words of explanation may not be out of place. To fill in the outlines were too much like writing the annals of a combination slaughter-house and honk-a-tonk. The Anglican Church came into being because the Pope would not divorce Henry VIII from a virtuous wife that he might marry Anne Boleyn—his own daughter by a disreputable drab! Because the Pope would not play Pandarus to Henry's unholy passion, the latter proclaimed himself the head of the Catholic Church in his Kingdom, made Cranmer his primate and Thomas Cromwell his vicar-general or chief gyasticutus. In the whole world there was but one man more brutal than Cranmer, and that was Cromwell; but one constitutionally meaner than Cromwell, and that was Cranmer; but one more bestial than either, and that was King Henry. And upon these three pillars rests the entire superstructure known as the Anglican Church, or Protestant Episcopalianism! Should Oofty Goofty, the Yellow Kid and the editor of the Houston *Post* essay a revision of the Code Napoleon or Justinian Pandects, it would be neither so impudent nor ridiculous as the attempt of this gallows-faced triumvirate of black-hearted rascals to bring about a religious "Reformation." Having in the meantime gotten Anne Boleyn with child, Henry secretly married her before obtaining a divorce, or even a semblance thereof, from Catherine, thereby becoming a bigamist as well as an adulterer. Henry had been criminally intimate with Anne Boleyn's mother, and we have it on the respectable authority of Dr. Bayley that she warned him previous to the marriage that his intended was his own daughter. Cranmer, who divorced Henry from Catherine, subsequently relieved him of Anne by declaring the marriage—which had been a second time solemnized—was of no effect, thereby bastardizing Elizabeth, the too-early fruit of the union. In this view both houses of parliament concurred, alleging the invalidity of his marriage with Anne "because of certain just and lawful impediments." These "certain just and lawful impediments" were urged by both Cranmer and the King, but they do not appear to have worried the pious pope of the Anglican Church until he caught daughter-wife dallying with the gentlemen of his household when she was charged, among other frailties, with incest with her brother, and promptly beheaded. The next day Henry was happily wedded to a new wife! And from such a source sprang the Anglican Church, which numbers Charles I among its "blessed martyrs," and has Bishop Coleman and Perry for apologists! The Episcopalians indignantly deny that Anne Boleyn was Henry's daughter; but that she was so, and that both she and Henry knew it at the time of their marriage, there is indisputable documentary evidence. Lady Elizabeth Boleyn, Anne herself, Cranmer and King Henry confessed the consanguineous relationship. Probably Lady Boleyn did not know to an absolute certainty who Anne's father was, any more than Anne knew for a surety who Elizabeth's father was; but in cases of this kind we must, perforce, accept the testimony of the mother as final. Lady Boleyn's daughter Mary was likewise the Anglican pope's leman; but one possible case of incest more or less on the part of such a great religious "reformer" is a matter of small importance. With the subsequent marriages, divorces and beheadings of the apostle of the Anglican faith we need not concern ourselves. They are familiar to everybody but Episcopalians.

Bigamy, incest, uxoricide and adultery are not the only crimes of which the founder of this new faith stands convicted. For nearly nine centuries England has been a Catholic country. The Church of Rome had transformed the English race from a race of barbarous root-diggers, who fled like scared rabbits before the legions of Caesar, into a nation at once civilized, prosperous and powerful. Crime and pauperism were practically unknown. It was the boast of an English king that jewels hung upon the trees by the roadside were safe as tho' encased in vaults of stone and iron; that within his realm there was no beggar, none suffering for shelter or bread. Beef, pork and mutton were described by pre-reformation historians as "the meat of the poor." This was the age in which Albion received the name of "merrie England," in which she won that reputation for hospitality and good cheer which for more than 300 years has been but a shadow of a shade. It was during this epoch that Ireland became famous as the seat of learning to which the crowned heads of Europe sent their sons. A considerable portion of the arable land of the two islands was owned by monasteries, their tenants enjoying almost freehold privileges. These monastic institutions educated the youth and cared for the aged. This was not alone their pleasure; it was their legal duty, for it was at that time recognized that the landlord held natural resources in trust; that every person, howsoever poor, was entitled to a subsistence from the soil. Judged by our present economic ideas, the system was bad; but with all our wisdom we have as yet been unable to put a system in practice that produced such beneficial effects. Good or ill, the system was there, the people had become accustomed to it, and the most callow kindergarten statesman knows that it is suicidal to violently subvert immemorial custom. Henry, having proclaimed himself the Anglican pope, despoiled the monastic institutions of their land, robbed their churches and divided the booty among his favorites, leaving no provision for the education of youth or the sustenance of age, thereby flooding the

Kingdom with ignorance, beggary and crime. Dr. Sharpe declares that the despoliation of the religious houses of London "caused the streets to be thronged with the sick and poor." Such was the immediate fruit of the Protestant "Reformation." From beef, pork and mutton being the "meat of the poor," labor in England began to live on black bread and water, in Ireland on water and boiled potatoes. During his lifetime this incestuous monster, aided by Cromwell and Cranmer, cruelly persecuted all those who refused to recognize his spiritual as well as his temporal supremacy. They invaded convents and tore down altars to secure gold and silver with which they were ornamented, ransacked chests and destroyed valuable books for the sake of the gilt binding. The monastery of St. Austin, called the Apostle of England, was plundered, the tomb of Thomas-a-Beckett despoiled of the pious offerings of pilgrims, and the sainted dust of the dead were hurled to the four winds of heaven. Protestant and Catholics were tied together in pairs, one of each, back to back, dragged through the streets and consigned to the flames as heretics. Priests and priors were hanged, drawn and quartered, their hearts and entrails cast into the fire, their bodies parboiled, their hands nailed up before the doors of monasteries as a warning that the paramour of Anne Boleyn would permit no trifling in matters of piety. Sir Thomas More, the most learned lawyer in the Kingdom, and Bishop Fisher, who had been the privy councillor of Henry's father, suffered death for declining to accept this bloody-minded butcher as God's vice-regent on earth! But enough! A magazine ten times the size of the Iconoclast would be thrice filled by printing in the smallest possible type the names of those who suffered death for no other reason than a positive refusal to apostatize. We may dismiss Thomas Cromwell, the new pope's vicar-general, in a paragraph: He was simply another brutal, ignorant Jack-the-Ripper. He seems to have been a servant in the household of Cardinal Wolsey, and by treachery to his old master recommended himself to the good graces of Henry. But Cranmer was a man of a different stripe—intellectual, foxy, ambitious. He is another "blessed martyr" of the Episcopalians. I will not trust myself to paint his portrait, for I despise the unctuous old scoundrel so heartily that I should do him injustice—if it were possible to heap upon the head of an imp of hell unmerited ignominy. I leave the labor of love to Macaulay, the hater of Catholicism, the eulogist of the "Establishment," the sweet singer of the glory of Elizabeth, England's virgin (?)

queen, feeling assured that he will let him down as easily as his conscience will allow:

> Cranmer rose into favor by serving Henry in the disgraceful affair of his first divorce. * * * * He attached himself to Cromwell (Thomas) while the fortunes of Cromwell flourished. He voted for cutting off Cromwell's head without a trial when the tide of royal favor turned. He conformed backward and forward as the king changed his mind. While Henry lived he assisted in condemning to the flames those who denied the doctrine of trans-substantiation. When Henry died he found out that the doctrine was false. He was, however, not at a loss for people to burn. The sanguinary intolerance of a man who thus wavered in his creed excites a loathing to which it is difficult to give vent without calling foul names. Equally false to political and religious obligations, he was first the tool of Somerset, and then the tool of Northumberland. When the former wished to put his own brother to death, without the semblance of a trial, he found a ready instrument in Cranmer.

And of such material are Episcopalian martyrs made. This is the party that helped Henry VIII establish the Anglican Church; this is the saint to whom our Episcopalian brethren are indebted for their Book of Common Prayer! This is he "of glorious memory," who, before the Anglican priesthood were permitted to marry, imported a wife from Germany, nailed up in a box, and while primate of the new church kept her concealed in his palace. Mary, Henry's legitimate daughter, was a Catholic. Fearing that if she ascended the throne she would compel them to restore the property of which they had despoiled the "Popists," the Godly, headed by Cranmer, attempted to change the succession, well knowing that to do so meant civil war. Failing in this, Cranmer and the rest of the canting crew, crawled to Mary's feet like abject curs. Cranmer recanted as a matter of course. Entirely of his own volition, he made six recantations in six weeks, each more pitiably abject than its predecessor. He declared that the doctrine he had enforced with gallows' ropes and branding irons and disemboweling hooks was false as hell, asked Mary's forgiveness and the prayers of the Pope. Finding that Mary was determined to make an example of him, he recanted his six recantations and died "a blessed martyr." The church planted by Henry VIII and Cromwell and Cranmer—triune of infamy!—was tenderly nurtured by "Sainted Edward VI," "Good Queen Bess" and "King Charles the Martyr." I am not writing a complete history of England just at present; but I'll just spike the gab-traps of those pious Episcopalians who have so much to say about "Bloody Mary." Like most other Protestants, I was taught early to believe that Queen Mary had scrambled Episcopalian brains for breakfast and slept with her bed floating in a vast tank of Puritan blood.

True, "Bloody Mary" burned old Cranmer; but as he was headed for hell anyhow, it was a mercy of acclimation. She made matters uncomfortable for several other people; but during her entire reign she caused fewer deaths for opinion's sake than did "the sainted Edward" in a single year. Where Mary let a drop of blood in the name of Catholicism, Elizabeth spilled a pint in defense of her own spiritual supremacy. Such is the testimony of the public records of England. I am not the apologist of either Queen Mary or St. Dominic. Catholic persecution is far more inexcusable than Protestant persecution, for the simple reason that the Mother Church is old enough to have learned wisdom. Its priests are usually learned men, and we have a right to expect better things of them than of the fanatical blatherskites who, like Sam Jones, were educated in a mule seminary, and who spout their religious theses from the tops of tubs. We can forgive Calvin for burning Servetus, for we can expect nothing better of a God-intoxicated savage with a scant thimbleful of sense; but Cranmer was a man of a different kidney, one who had brains and erudition in abundance. Luther was a man of some learning, but of disordered intellect. Were he living today, he would be adjudged insane and sent to the asylum. The assumption that he was crazy is the mildest construction that can be placed against his performances. Having rebelled against Rome because of its "indulgences," he proceeded to grant a more remarkable indulgence than the worst of Catholic prelates ever dreamed of. He authorized Philip of Hesse to have two wives at the same time—"in order to provide for the welfare of his body and soul, and to bring greater glory to God!" Although Luther did and Cranmer did not sanction polygamy, no one who has carefully studied the character of the two men will believe for a moment that Henry could have made of the first an obsequious pander to his passions. Luther was a religious crank, an ill-balanced, irresponsible enthusiast; Cranmer was a subtle plotter, an unprincipled scoundrel. And the difference between the representative men of the opposing sects extended to their disciples. The Puritans persecuted because they were, as a rule, ignorant men who had been wrought up into a religious frenzy; the Anglican Church persecuted with a view to political power and pecuniary profit. I have said that Luther was crazy; but his opinion of Henry VIII well-nigh destroys that hypothesis. He declared that the founder of the Anglican Church was "a pig, an ass, a dunghill, the spawn of an adder, a basilisk, a lying buffoon, a mad fool with a frothy mouth and a w——h face"—which demonstrates that, like Hamlet, he could tell a hawk from a heron-saw when the wind was in the right direction.

"Bloody Mary"—whose victims numbered less than 300 all told, including Cranmer and numerous other rogues whom the world could well spare—was succeeded by Elizabeth, Anne Boleyn's scrawny brat. To her dying queen she swore to adhere ever to the Church of Rome, and prayed that the earth might open and swallow her up if she broke her vow. Her coronation oath made her defender of the Catholic faith, yet she was scarce seated upon the throne ere she apostatized. It must be comforting to Episcopalians to reflect that for five and forty years their church had a she-pope, a vinegar-hearted old virago who turned her palace into a den of vice. Faunt says at her court "all enormities reigned in the highest degree." Lingard avers that she assigned to her favorite paramour "an apartment contiguous to her own bedchamber, and by this indecent act proved that she had become regardless of her character and callous to every sense of shame. The court," he naively adds, "imitated the manners of the sovereign." And for nearly half a century this was the Anglican Vatican—with Dudley, Raleigh, Blount, Oxford, Anjou, Simier, Hatton, *et id genus omnes* as College of Cardinals! Under such happy auspices the H'english Church was brought to its present state of perfection—flourished like a green bay 'orse! Old Liz seems to have persecuted Puritan and Catholic with rigid impartiality, and a cruelty scarce equaled by Cranmer. Her favorite method of dealing with men who denied her spiritual supremacy was to hang them up until half dead, then rip out their bowels with grappling hooks. This was "Good Queen Bess," that "Virgin Queen" to accommodate whose sexual idiosyncrasies parliament decreed that any brat she might happen to have, by whatsoever syndicate of sires, should succeed to the sceptre. But the act was useless—the cake had too many cooks. In those days a man couldn't loll around in slippers and dressing gown on Sunday morning and peruse the papers. So deeply consecrated was the Queen for his immortal soul that if he failed to show up at her church she fined him 20 pounds for the first offense, and kept doubling the dose. If that failed to bring the contumacious sinner to time she sawed off his head and flung his internal economy into the fire. Her pursuivants burst into private houses at any hour of the day or night and ransacked them from top to bottom for "Popish" paraphernalia, and woe betide that unlucky wight whose possessions suggested the Papal See! She crammed the prisons with recusants, confiscated their estates and kept the rack, the gibbet and the persuasive bowel-hooks in constant operation "for the greater glory of God!" Cobbett says:

> One greedy and merciless minion after another was sent to Ireland to goad that devoted people to acts of desperation, and that too, not only for the obvious purpose, but for the avowed purpose, of obtaining a pretense for new confiscations. The "Reformation" from its very outset had plunder written on its front; but as to Ireland it was all plunder, from the crown of its head to the sole of its foot. This horrible lynx-like she-tyrant could not watch each movement of the Catholics there as she did in England. She could not harass them in detail; therefore she murdered them in masses.

This is but a glimpse of the portrait of "Good Queen Bess," as drawn by the pen of a Protestant. That this little sketch of the founders of Episcopalianism might be eminently conservative, I have excluded the testimony of Catholics and Puritans, the objects of their persecution. It is doubtful if all the savage atrocities perpetrated by the followers of Knox and Calvin, added to all the cruelties chargeable to the Catholics in every age and clime, would equal the outrages sanctioned by this red-headed old harlot in less than half a century. There have been bone-breakings and tongue-borings and burnings by Puritans and by Catholics; but they were the result of mistaken zeal; those perpetrated by the Anglican Church have not that excuse. It were an insult to common sense to urge that an old wife-butcher like Henry, a bawd like Elizabeth, a liar like Charles had any genuine regard for religion or morals. What Puritans and Catholics inflicted they were willing to suffer—and frequently did suffer—rather than recant; but look at Cranmer and the rest of that unclean crew who have persecuted in the name of the law-established Church of England—not a man of whom but was ready to recant at a moment's notice to save his worthless neck, or for his pecuniary profit! Queen Mary was always a Catholic. To preserve her faith she defied her unnatural half-brother and her still more unnatural father. The one threatened her life, the other disinherited her; but to her life and crown were as nothing to the chrism and the cross. Elizabeth was a devout Protestant when Edward VI was persecuting Catholics, and an equally devout Catholic when Mary was persecuting Protestants. Branded by Parliament as an illegitimate, and tacitly acknowledging herself a strumpet in consenting to the act of "natural" succession, this old heifer was for nearly half a century the "Anglo-Saxons'" first lady of the land! No wonder Englishmen assume airs of superiority

—that Episcopalianism has become such a hot favorite with our own Anglomaniacs. It is not every church that can trace its lineage back in an unbroken line to the amours of Anne Boleyn and 'Andsome 'Arry! Every man to his taste; but I prefer crazy Luther, who says he slept with the devil, to Henry, who wedded with his daughter; St. Dominic's thumbscrews for heretics to "Good Queen Bess' " disemboweling hooks. I really don't care to mix up with a family of religious reformers in which a fellow is likely to discover he's his own grandfather.

Elizabeth shone like Luna, by borrowed light. The glories of her age are not her glories. During her reign English literature reached its zenith and gilded her throne with an adventitious glory. It was the high noon of intellect; but it was the twilight of religion and the midnight of morality. The Augustan Age was not that of Rome's political glory or commercial greatness, but the beginning of her decay. Those brilliant minds that made the times of Elizabeth memorable were the fruitage of kindly Catholic culture. You may trace British literature from the days of Alfred, step by step, onward and upward, to that imperial height where Shakespeare lifts his brow, bound with the anademe of immortality—but beyond him is the blank abyss! The fruit of the Elizabethan Era was Apples of Hesperides, but the tree was dead! The accursed "Reformation" of King Henry had pauperized the once fruitful soil and withdrawn the kindly dews; it lifted its leafless branches into a leaden sky and struck its withered roots into rocks and ashes. The founders of the Anglican Church left England bankrupt, both in money and brains. When Henry VIII ascended the throne it was a powerful and prosperous nation; by the time it was done with "Charles the blessed Martyr" it was little better—if we may believe Lingard, Cobbett, Lever and others—than a congeries of criminals, beggars and bawds. It declined in wealth and power until the Puritans kicked the immortal ichor out of the "Establishment." Under the Lord Protector it regained somewhat of its old-time political prestige, only to sink still lower when the Anglican religion was re-established. The regime of "Old Noll" was doubtless fantastic, cruel and despotic; but he made the flag of England again respected in every land and on every sea. If he devastated Scotland and Ireland, he humbled Holland and Spain. He was the father of England's maritime greatness and of her colonial empire. We hear a great deal of "glorious Queen Bess;" but what she contributed to England's greatness other than, by her meddling, to provoke the so-called "massacre of St. Bartholomew" in France, and by her treachery, to bring the Spanish Armada down upon her poverty-stricken shores and escape destruction only by the intervention of a storm, I do not now remember.

If the reign of the Puritans was savage, it was because the long-continued cruelties and innate cussedness of the Anglican church had made men mad. Those who had had their ears clipped and their noses slit; those whose property had been confiscated and their relatives butchered by Charles, could scarce be expected to cast bouquets at him and his henchmen when they got the inhuman hyenas grabbed. The Episcopalians have no cause to complain of the Puritans. They were the natural sequence, the inevitable result of Henry's "Reformation." When he broke away from the authority of Rome he unloosed a power which he could not control. By his rebellion against the Pope he proclaimed the right of private judgment. He started the avalanche but could not stop it. If one man might ignore the the spiritual authority of Pope Clement, others might, with even greater propriety, deny the spiritual supremacy of King Henry. Finally his bastard Catholico-Protestantism degenerated into Puritanism, and the throne of Britain, like Frankenstein, was destroyed by a monster of its own making. Had old Henry kept his concupiscence under control, there would have been no Protestant Episcopal Church to transform American hermaphrodites into Anglomaniacs, no illegitimate Elizabeths or "blessed Charles the Martyr." Protestantism and Catholicism would have met in a fair field in Britain as they did in America. Men would have adopted one or the other, instead of a compound of both, acceptable to neither Deity nor Devil—a religious mulatto or moral mule. Tens of thousands of lives would have been saved. England would not boast a few great fortunes, offset by a million registered paupers; and Ireland, fruitful as the gardens of the gods, be a synonym for poverty and suffering. I trust that Bishops Coleman and Perry will pardon the suggestion that, as Anne Boleyn's beauty was the inspiration of Episcopalianism, its divine revelation, so to speak, and as she was the first to die for its sake, she should have the post of honor in its hagiology.

THE BEAUTEOUS REBECCA

A Billet D'Amour

Trivial perhaps, but this article and the one following reflect, in Brann's sarcastic best, the amazing dislike he had long nurtured for his one-time associate, Rienzi M. Johnston, editor of the Houston Post.

Miss Rebecca Merlindy Johnston, Care Post, Houston, Tex.

My Erstwhile Own:—Pardon me, Merlindy, dear, for addressing you thro' the columns of a great religious journal, instead of slipping my tender billy-doo under your back gate by the melancholy light of the gibbous moon. Conditions have arisen in this unkind and captious age which make it necessary that I should hang my torn heart upon my sleeve for daws to peck at, instead of following the lead of my soulful longings and enclosing my viscera in an antique envelope, perfumed with frangipanna, and firing it at my Merlindy thro' the mails. You know—or I will grant you do—the poet says, "What great ones do the less will prattle of." They are prattling of you and I Merlindy. In the first flush of our fond affections we did forget that fixed upon us was the curious gaze of the *hoi polloi,* and ere we were aware Dame Rumor had donned her Sunday gown and sailed abroad to pour into the prurient public ear another tale of a trusting maid undone by selfish man—had even hinted that you were playing Madeline to my Willie. 'Twas all my fault. You were so pure and unsuspecting, so little versed in the ways of this wicked world, and I should have guarded you with the thoughtful solicitude of a careful shepherd shielding from a sneaping frost the fresh-dropped female lamb. I should not have permitted you to patter about the public streets in male attire and call yourself Rienzi Miltiades—I should have bade you beware those cute little breeches and that bobtail coat.

Heaven forfend that I should be the unhappy cause of your spotless character being called in question. God wotteth well that your fair name and fame are dearer to me than the ruddy drops that visit my sad heart. (See Donnelly's Cryptogram.) But you are not bearing yourself toward me in a manner to allay suspicion. The public is quick to see the similitude of your treatment of the Apostle and Miss Pollard's haughty scorn of her former paramour, and is hinting that like causes produce like effects—is even putting its tongue in its larboard cheek and suggesting that "Hell hath no fury like a woman scorned." But don't you believe, Merlindy, that the Apostle scorns you. He knows your worth, and will stick to you, thro' good and evil report, like a dead game sport to loaded dice.

> "My pen is pore, my ink is pail,
> But love for you shall never fale."

Tho' you have ceased to love me, and decline to be even a sister to me, I cannot forget those dear old days that are dead, before "Pinkie" of the Hill tribes crept into our ambrosial Eden like the odor of Buffalo Bayou into the boudoir of a Houston belle. You should be more cautious, Merlindy. You should remember that the public is watching you as intently as a nigger preacher eyes the plug hat circulated for the capture of small coin. Tho' your heart may break tomorrow you must be all smiles tonight. If you desire to spill your fond affections on a blond vacuum chained to an Aurora Borealis you should do it unostentatiously, and thereby dodge the damning suspicion that your life is wrecked and that you are throwing away the fragments in a fit of hilarious desperation. You should not advertise the fact that you turn the hose on me when I seek to warble some pathetic roundelay or work off an Ella Wheeler yearn under your dormer window. You should not bruit it abroad that you whistle on your lily-white fingers for the police when I attempt to unbosom my pent-up agony to the sympathetic moon in your back yard.

Rebecca Merlindy, my soulful bird of Paradise, if you have really soured on me—if our ecstatic yum-yum was too intoxicatingly sweet for a steady diet—I shall not upbraid you; but you should not with your dainty tootsie-wootsies, trample on a true heart, nor play fast and loose with a pure affection that has unwittingly warped itself about your lovely diaphragm like a boa-constrictor encircling a yearling calf. You have a right to discard me, Rebecca; but no right to drive me to drink by turning up your patrician gold-cure nose as I pass humbly by, then filling the white horse moustache of Epictetus Paregoric Hill with hyblaean honey.

But I will not complain. 'Twere better to have loved and lost than ne'er to have loved at all. Instead of hanging my harp on the willows I will attune it to the soul-sob key and pour forth my sad lament like the bulbul warbling to the red, red rose, while she presses the cruel thorn ever deeper into her wounded heart. I will return good for evil, because I am built that way. Instead of answering scorn with scorn, as little souls would do, I will bend all my poor talents and wobbly energies to the holy task of making you immortal. And I will succeed, or burst a suspender in the sacred enterprise. I will dramatize our tale of true love turned awry, and "Pinkie" shall play the heavy villain—shall hypnotize you with the splendor of his sunset hair and make you err against your better judgment. I will weave you into song and story like a thread of burnished gold in a somber carpet of rags, or a clean cuspidore in a Populist sanctum. The ages yet to be shall remember you as the Apostle's sweetheart, even as the present recalls the Laura of Petrarch, the Heloise of Abelard and the Dulcinea of Don Quixote. Tho' parted in life we will be united in death. Posterity will attend to that—will scoop together our pathetic dust and plant it in some romantic spot, where the shadow of the quivering aspen falls and the bull-frog's melancholy croak makes life not worth the living. And every lover throughout the wide, wide world whose affection has slipped its trolley-pole, will come apilgriming as to some sacred shrine, pull off an unpainted picket and drop upon our lowly mound the sympathetic sob and scalding tear.

Ah, Merlindy, you may not be so beautiful as Ida Wells, nor so intellectual as Mrs. Lease; but my soulful song shall so gloss your imperfections o'er that in the unborn ages yet to be you'll loom up on the sensuous cigarette or soothing "hardware" sign a very Hebe, and no living picture exhibit will be complete without some counterfeit presentment of your personal pulchritude, attired in hand-me-down pants. Adios, but not farewell.

"THE APOSTLE"

WOMAN'S WICKEDNESS

Brann tended generally to idealize womankind in his writings. But he favored the viewpoint that as woman was capable of a higher plane than man, she could also, conversely, fall lower.

By the "social evil" is commonly understood illicit intercourse of the sexes, a violation of law or custom intended to regulate the procreative passion.

The "evil" is probably as old as society, coeval with mankind. History—tradition itself—goes not back to a time when statutes, confessedly human, or professedly divine, were capable of controlling the fierce fires that blaze within the blood—when all-consuming Love was cold Reason's humble slave and Passion yielded blind obedience unto Precept. Although the heavens have been ever peopled with threatening gods and the great inane filled with gaping hells; although kings and courts have thundered their inhibitions forth, and society turned upon illicit love Medusa's awful frown, the Paphian Venus has flourished in every age and clime, and still flaunts her scarlet flag in the face of heaven.

The history of humanity—its poetry, its romance, its very religion—is little more than a Joseph's coat, woven of Love's celestial warp and Passion's infernal woof in the loom of Time. For sensuous Cleopatra's smiles Mark Antony thought the world was lost; for false Helen's favors proud Ilion's temples blazed, and the world is strewn with broken altars and ruined fanes, with empty crowns and crumbling thrones blasted by the selfsame curse.

In many cities of every land abandoned women are so numerous, despite all these centuries of law-making and moralizing, that they find it impossible to earn a livelihood by their nefarious trade—are driven by sheer necessity to seek more respectable employment. The supply of public prostitutes is apparently limited only by the demand, while the number of "kept women" is constantly increasing, and society becoming day by day more lenient to those favorites of fortune who have indulged in little escapades not in strict accord with the Seventh Commandment. It is now a common occurrence for a female member of the "Four Hundred" who has confessedly gone astray, to be received back on an equality with her most virtuous sisters. In ancient Sparta theft was considered proper, but getting caught a crime. Modern society has improved upon that peculiar moral code. Adultery—if the debauchee have wealth—is but a venial fault, and to be found out a trifling misfortune, calling for condolence rather than condemnation. It is not so much the number of professed prostitutes that alarms the student of sociology, as the brutal indifference to even the semblance of sexual purity which is taking possession of our social aristocracy, and which poison, percolating through the underlying strata, threatens to eliminate womanly continence from the world.

If, despite all our safeguards of law and the restraining force of religion, society becomes more hopelessly corrupt; if, with our advancing civilization, courtesans increase in number; if, with our boasted progress in education and the arts, women of alleged respectability grow less chary of their charms—if the necessities of poverty and the luxury of wealth alike breed brazen bawds and multiply cuckolds—it is a fair inference that there is something radically wrong with our social system.

It might be well, perhaps, for priests and publicists to cease launching foolish anathemas and useless statutes at prostitution long enough to inquire what is driving so many bright young women into dens of infamy,—for those good souls who are laboriously striving to drag their fallen sisters out of the depths, to study the causes of the disease before attempting a cure. I say disease, for I cannot agree with those utilitarians who profess to regard prostitution as a "necessary evil;" who protest that the brute passions of man must be sated,—that but for the Scarlet Woman he would debauch the Vestal Virgin. I do not believe that Almighty God decreed that one-half the women of this world should be sacrificed upon the unclean altar of Lust that the others might be saved . It is an infamous, a revolting doctrine, a damning libel of the Deity. All the courtesans beneath heaven's blue concave never caused a single son of Adam's misery to refrain from tempting, so far as he possessed the power, one virtuous woman. Never.

Governor Fishback, of Arkansas, recently declared that "houses of ill-fame are necessary to city life," and added: "If you close these sewers of men's animal passions you overflow the home and spread disaster."

This theory has been adopted by many municipalities, courtesans duly licensed, their business legitimatized and accorded the protection of the law. If houses of ill-fame be "necessary to city life;" if they prevent the overflow of the home of bestial lust and the spread of disaster, it follows as a natural sequence that the prostitute is a public benefactor, to be encouraged rather than condemned, deserving of civic honor rather than social infamy. Will Governor Fishback and his fellow utilitarians be kind enough to make a careful examination of the quasi-respectable element of society and inform us how large an army of courtesans will be necessary to enable it to pass a baking powder purity test?

Governor Fishback does not appear to have profited by Pope's suggestion that "The proper study of mankind is man," or he would know full well that the presence in a city of prostitutes but serves to accentuate the dangers that environ pure womanhood. He would know that they add fuel to Lust's unholy fires, that thousands of them are procuresses as well as prostitutes, and that one bad woman can do more to corrupt her sex than can any libertine since the days of Sir Launcelot. He would likewise know that so perverse is the nature of man that he would leave a harem filled with desirous houris more beautiful than ever danced through Mohammedan dream of Paradise, to dig pitfalls for the unwary feet of some misshapen country wench who was striving to lead an honest life. As muley cow will turn from a manger filled with new-mown hay, and wear out her thievish tongue trying to coax a wisp of rotten straw through a crack in a neighbor's barn, so will man turn from consenting Venus' matchless charms to solicit scornful Dian.

What is it that is railroading so large a portion of the young women to hell? What causes so many to forsake the "straight and narrow path" that is supposed to lead to everlasting life, and seek the irremediable way of eternal death? What mad phantasy is it that leads so many wives to sacrifice the honor of their husbands and shame their children? Is it evil inherent in the daughters of Eve themselves? Is it lawless lust or force of circumstances that adds legion after legion to the cohorts of shame? Or has our boasted progress brought with it a suspicion that female chastity is, after all, an overprized bauble—that what is no crime against nature should be tolerated by this eminently practical age? We have cast behind us the myths and miracles, proven the absurdity of our ancestors' most cherished traditions and brought their idols beneath the iconoclastic hammer. In this general social and intellectual house-cleaning have we consigned virtue to the rubbish heap—or at least relegated it to the garret with the spinning-wheel, hand-loom and other out of date trumpery? Time was when a woman branded as a bawd hid her face for shame, or consorted only with her kind; now, if she can but become sufficiently notorious she goes upon the stage, and men take their wives and daughters to see her play "Camille" and kindred characters. This may signify much; among other things that the courtesan is creeping into social favor—even that a new code of morals is now abuilding, in which she will be the grand exemplar. As change is the order of the day, and what one age damns its successor ofttimes deifies, who knows but an up-to-date religion may yet be evolved with Bacchic revels for sacred rites and a favorite prostitute for high priestess?

Were I called upon to diagnose the social disease; did any duly ordained committee—from the numerous "Reform" societies, Ministerial Associations, secular legislatures or other bodies that are taking unto themselves great credit for assiduously making a bad matter worse—call upon me for advice anent the proper method of restoring to healthy life the word's moribund morality, I would probably shock the souls out of them by stating a few plain facts without troubling myself to provide polite trimmings.

You cannot reform society from the bottom; you must begin at the top.

Man, physically considered, is merely an animal, and the law of his life is identical with that of the brute creation. Continence in man or woman is a violation of nature's edicts, a sacrifice made by the individual to the necessities of civilization.

Like the beast of the field, man formerly took upon himself a mate, and with his rude strength defended her from the advances of other males. Such, reduced to the last analysis, is the basis of marriage, of female chastity and family honor. Rape and adultery were prohibited under pains and penalties, and behind the sword of the criminal law grew up the moral code. As wealth increased man multiplied his wives and added concubines; but woman was taught that while polygamy was pleasing to the gods polyandry was the reverse—that while the husband was privileged to seek sexual pleasure in a foreign bed, the wife who looked with desiring eyes upon other than her rightful lord merited the scorn of earth and provoked the wrath of heaven.

For long ages woman was but the creature of man's caprice, the drudge or ornament of his house, mistress of neither her body nor her mind. But as the world advanced and matter was made more subject unto mind—as divine Reason wrested the sceptre from brute Force—woman began to assume her proper place in the world's economy. She is stepping forth into the garish light of freedom, is realizing for the first time in the history of the human race that she is a moral entity—that even she, and not another, is the arbiter of her fate. And, as ever before, new-found freedom is manifesting itself in criminal folly—liberty has become a synonym for license.

The "progressive" woman—the woman who is not only well "up-to-date," but skirmishing with the future—is asking her brother: "If thou, why not I? If man is forgiven a score of mistresses must woman, blessed with like reason and cursed with kindred passions, be damned for one lover?" And while the question grates upon her ear, the answer comes not trippingly to the tongue. I do not mean that all women who imagine themselves progressive are eager to assume the same easy morals that from time immemorial have characterized the sterner sex; but this line of argument, peculiar to their class, while not likely to make men better, is well calculated to make foolish women worse. The sooner they realize that he-Dians are scarce in the country as brains in the head of a chrysanthemum dude; that such sexual purity as the world is to be blessed withal must be furnished by the softer sex, the better for all concerned. That they will eventually cease their altogether useless clamor that bearded men become as modest as blushing maids, and agree with the poet that "Whatever is, is right," the lessons of history bid us hope. When the French people threw off the yoke of the royalist and aristocrat they likewise loudly clamored for equality, fraternity and other apparently reasonable but utterly impossible things, until the bitter school of experience taught them better. The progressive women have not yet set up la Belle Guillotine—in Washington or elsewhere—for the decapitation of male incorrigibles; which significant fact confirms our old faith that the ladies rather like a man who would not deliberately overdo the part of Joseph.

But the female "reformer," with her social board of equalization theories, is but a small factor in that mighty force which is filling the land with unfaithful wives and the potter's field with degraded prostitutes.

When the people of a nation are almost universally poor, sexual purity is the general rule. Simple living and severe toil keep in check the passions and make it possible to mould the mind with moral precepts. But when a nation becomes divided into the very rich and the extremely poor; when wilful Waste and woeful Want go hand in hand; when luxury renders abnormal passions of the one; and cupidity, born of envy, blunts the moral perceptions of the other, then indeed is that nation delivered over to the world, the flesh and the devil. When all alike are poor, contentment reigns. The son grows up a useful, self-reliant man, the daughter an industrious virtuous woman. From this class comes nearly every benefactor of mankind. It has ever been the great repository of morality, the balance-wheel of society, the brain and brawn of the majestic world. Divided into millionaires and mendicants, the poor man's son becomes feverish to make a showy fortune by fair means or by foul, while his daughter looks on with envious eye upon m'lady, follows her fashions and too often apes her morals. The real life is supplanted by the artificial, and people are judged, not by what they are, but by what they have. The "true-love match" becomes but a reminiscence—the blind god's bow is manipulated by brutish Mammon. Men and women make "marriages of convenience," consult their fortunes rather than their affections—seek first a lawful companion with a well-filled purse, and then a congenial paramour.

The working girl soon learns that beyond a few stale platitudes—fired off much as a hungry man says grace—she gets no more credit for wearing honest rags than flaunting dishonest silks; that good name, however precious it may be to her, is really going out of fashion—that when the world pretends to prize it above rubies it is lying—is indulging in the luxury of hypocrisy. She likewise learns that the young men really worth marrying, knowing that a family means a continual striving to be fully as fashionable and artificial as those better able to play the fool, seek mistresses rather than wives. She becomes discouraged, desperate, and drifts into the vortex.

Much is said by self-constituted reformers of the lachrymose school anent trusting maids "betrayed" by base-hearted scoundrels, and loving wives led astray by designing villains; but I could never work my sympathies up to the slopping over stage for these pathetic victims of man's perfidy. It may be that my tear-glands lack a hair-trigger attachment, and my sob-machine is not of the most approved pattern. Perchance woman is fully as big a fool as these reformers paint her—that she has no better sense than a blind horse that has been taught to yield a ready obedience to any master—to submit itself without question to the guidance of any hand. Will the "progressive" woman—who is just now busy boycotting Col. Breckinridge and spilling her salt tears over his discarded drab—kindly take a day off and tell us what is to become of this glorious country when such incorrigible she-idiots get control of it? It is well enough to protect the honor of children with severe laws and a double-shotted gun; but the average young woman is amply able to guard her virtue if she really values it, while the married woman who becomes so intimate with a male friend that he dares assail her continence, deserves no sympathy. She is the tempter, not the victim. True it is that maids, and matrons too, as pure as the white rose that blooms above the green glacier, have been swept too far by the fierce whirlwind of love and passion; but of these the world doth seldom hear. The woman whose sin is sanctified by love—who staked her name and fame upon a cowardly lie masquerading in the garb of eternal truth—never yet rushed into court with her tale of woe or aired her grievance in the public prints. The world thenceforth can give but one thing she wants, and that's an unmarked grave. May God in his mercy shield all such from the parrot criticisms and brutal insults of the fish-blooded, pharisaical female, whose heart never thrilled to love's wild melody, yet who marries for money—puts her frozen charms up at auction for the highest bidder, and having obtained a fair price by false pretenses, imagines herself pre-eminently respectable! In the name of all the gods at once, which is the fouler crime, the greater "social evil:" For a woman to deliberately barter her person for gold and lands, for gew-gaws, social position and a preferred pew in a fashionable church—even though the sale be in accordance with law, have the benediction of a stupid priest and the sanction of a corrupt and canting world—or, in defiance of custom and forgetful of cold precept, to cast the priceless jewel of a woman's honor upon the altar of illicit love?

Give the latter woman a chance, forget her fault, and she will become a blessing to society, an ornament to heaven; the former is fit inhabitant only for a hell of ice. She has deliberately dishonored herself, her sex and the man whose name she bears, and Custom can no more absolve her than the pope can pardon sin. She is the most dreadful product of the "Social Evil," of unhallowed sexual commerce—is the child of Mammon and Medusa, the blue-ribbon abortion of this monster-bearing age.

A CARNIVAL OF CRIME

The author's ever-appropriate plaint against the law's delay.

During the year 1894 there were about 9,800 homicides and but 132 legal executions reported in the United States. I have no later statistics at hand; but it is conceded, I believe, that crimes of this kind are steadily on the increase, while the disproportion between the number of homicides and hangings continues to grow greater. As matters now stand, one might slay a fellow mortal every year and stand an excellent chance of dying of old age, so far as the courts are concerned. You may go upon the streets, insult a man, provoke him to offer you violence, shoot him down like a dog, and, if able to employ eminent counsel to behedge you with legal technicalities and befuddle the jury, go scot free; or failing in that, put the public to an expense of several thousand dollars in excess of what your cowardly carcass is worth, and escape with a short term in some comfortable penitentiary, where you will be well cared for, taught a good trade and regularly prayed for at the expense of law-abiding people. What is the result? The people, despairing of legal protection from the armed thug, take the law into their own hands—invoke the power of Judge Lynch to defend their right to life, liberty and the pursuit of happiness. There are more lynchings than legal executions. In 1894 the first reached the appalling number of 190. That is indeed a terrible record of lawless violence, but it were idle to declaim against the effect without removing the cause. The American people are naturally law-abiding; but above and beyond their respect for courts is their inherent sense of justice—paramount even to the law of the land is the law of self-preservation. Theorists may protest and sentimentalists rend their nether garments and spill their ready tears; but so long as the assassin is white-washed by the courts and the rape-fiend turned loose to prey upon pure homes, Judge Lynch will continue to roar in the hands of maddened mobs and the lonely tree groan beneath its gruesome burden. Is it any wonder that the people lose patience? In Judge Lynch's court there is no eminent counsel skilled in the esoteric art of protecting crime; no change of venue; no mistrials; no appeals; no postponements to give important witnesses time to die or get away; no one-year terms in the penitentiary for the brutal assassin or infamous rape-fiend. We have "reformed" our jurisprudence until the contention of the courts with the great tide of crime suggests Dame Partington's unequal combat with the sea. By assiduously trundling her mop she was able to fill her bucket with brine; and by laboriously grinding, the courts succeed in cramming the penitentiaries—with small-fry thieves and people too poor to employ skilled counsel. Our courts have become mere circumlocution offices, winding and unwinding red tape, instead of the sinewy arm of justice wielding the unerring sword. Our judges are usually learned and upright, our juries eager to administer justice, our officers active and the public heart in the right place; but it avails not—our system is all wrong. We make too many laws, then involve them in a mass of legal verbiage which permits a skilled sophist to demonstrate to the untrained mind that they mean what best serves the interest of his client. It is common cant that "the people make the laws." They do not. The lawyers make them, and that with the full understanding that the more intricate the legal machinery may be, the more need of experts, the fatter the harvest of fees. All the criminal laws this country needs could be printed in a pamphlet no larger than the Iconoclast, together with full instructions for their enforcement; made so plain that the most stupid juror could understand them—and in simplicity there is strength. "Thou shalt not kill," says the Bible; and the sentence stands out like a star. The penalty for violation of this law was death, unless it plainly appeared that the killing was accidental or done in self-defense. The trial was immediate, and, if conviction followed, the culprit turned over to the "avenger of blood." No provision for experts to pass upon the sanity of the prisoner, no prattle of hypnotism, no searching of the community for the greatest numskulls to determine the case, no reversals on legal technicalities, no penitentiary and convict labor problem—no lawyers! A careful, common sense inquiry, honorable acquittal or conviction and immediate execution. The jury constitutes the chief feature of our legal machinery, a feature in full accord with our theory of popular sovereignty; but we have so hedged it about with foolish restrictions that, instead of being the ancillary of Justice, it has become a veritable bulwark of Crime. We select as jurors, not those who know most about the case, but those who know least. When an atrocious crime is committed we set aside as unavailable those who have kept in touch with current events, and select a jury from the residue. In these days of rapid transit and daily papers all men of average intelligence are soon informed of every crime of consequence committed in their county, even in their State; and no one gifted with a thinking apparatus can avoid arriving at some conclusion regarding all he sees and hears. As a rule, we get together twelve of the most consummate blockheads in the county—a dime museum of mental freaks—permit them to be further obfuscated by artful counsel, whose business it is to "make out a case" for or against, as goes the fee, then lock them up until the most obstinate jackass in the corral dominates the herd or compels a compromise. Sometimes there are two or more burros of equal obstinancy; a mistrial results, and the case goes over to the next term of court. The public loses interest in it—is absorbed in the contemplation of new crimes—and if the culprit is eventually convicted and properly punished the people regard it as a special dispensation of Providence. Punishment, to have a repressive effect, must be not only sure but swift. The law's delay—coupled with its uncertainty—encourages crime. More than five years ago, and on several occasions since then, the Iconoclast suggested that jurors be elected by the people like other county officers—that every county select nine men of approved worth to try criminal cases, and establish the majority rule. This would relieve the citizen of a disagreeable duty for which he is often in no wise qualified, and insure for jury service men capable of analyzing evidence and arriving at just conclusions. Let the vote of the jury in criminal cases be made a matter of public record, and thereby fix the responsibility for every miscarriage of justice. Only attorneys employed by the State should be permitted to appear in criminal cases. These should be skilled lawyers, but in no sense prosecuting attorneys, intent only upon securing conviction and pocketing a comfortable fee. Their business should be to elicit facts for the jury to pass upon, and act as counsellors to the court in questions of law. The attorney who will, with equal readiness, employ his skill to acquit a felon or hang an innocent man, should speedily become a forgotten factor in our criminal jurisprudence. In March, 1895, I called attention to these needed reforms, and well-nigh in the same words; but a question involving the lives of 10,000 Americans annually cannot be too frequently called to the attention of our publicists and the people.

JONAH'S GOURD

A biblical item, with the frequent appearance of but rude parody, while withal a fair sample of the Iconoclast's slapstick style.

Circumstances over which he seems to have had no control made Jonah the prototype of the modern panic-builder; *facile princeps* of chronic kickers, the high priest of professional calamity howlers. He received a call to cry against Ninevah because of its cussedness, but seems to have had a presentment that the job wouldn't pay, and made a desperate attempt to jump it. We are not advised what awful wickedness the city planted by Ninus and watered by Sennacherib had been guilty of. Perhaps a Democratic Congress had declined to add $500,000,000 to the interest-bearing burden of the people for the special behoof of the plutocracy. The people may have blasphemed the Golden Calf, declared for the money of the constitution, or hinted that they were better off when wrestling with the flesh-pots of Republicanism than trailing a mugwump king across barren deserts to a Babylonian captivity. Or they may have neglected to give the first fruits and fat of the land to the Lord—via the larders of the Levites. Certain it is that Nineveh had gotten off on the wrong foot, and Jonah was sent to "cry against it" and enable it to strike the proper gait. Like all the Jews of his generation, Jonah supposed that Jehovah ruled over but a small territory—that by crossing a State line he could get beyond his jurisdiction and into the bailiwick of other gods; so he boarded a packet plying between Joppa and Tarshish and "fled from the face of the Lord." It did not occur to the good man that Jehovah might have an extradition treaty with the Tarshish deity, or that he might make an excursion into foreign territory and recapture the runaway at the imminent risk of precipitating a celestico-international complication. Jonah probably did not suppose that Jehovah was cooped up in the Ark of the Covenant like the fisherman's genie in the vessel of copper, and uncorked only when the enemies of Israel became troublesome or some new people were to be despoiled of their corn and cattle, their vines and virgins; still, he imagined, like many people of the present day, that the Almighty clung pretty close to the amen-corner. But before the patron saint of amateur fishermen and professional falsifiers could get clear of the legal three-mile coast limit of Israel's God, that potentate pulled down on him with a double-barreled hurricane and a muzzle-loading leviathan. The aim was true, and Jonah tumbled. When he found himself in the belly of the big fish our peripatetic prophet from Galilee—which appears to have been the ancient Georgia—repented of his sins. We all do when they fail to pay the expected dividends. Jonah decided that he would rather go to Nineveh and found a Cleveland calamity club than travel, a perpetual passenger, in the prototype of Jules Verne's Nautilus; so he offered up penitential prayers, made fair promises and was permitted to go ashore.

"The Lord spake to the fish and it vomited Jonah upon dry land."

Pictures of the prophet walking ashore, with the lower jaw of the whale for gang-plank, are quite plentiful; but his remarks on that occasion have not been preserved. The kodak fiend seems to have been waiting for him, but the ubiquitous interviewer failed to get in his graft. Perhaps it is just as well; but it gives us a poor opinion of ancient journalism. During the three days and nights the prophet was a cabin passenger his whaleship must have swallowed a vast variety of the denizens of the deep, and it were interesting to know if Jonah lived happily with them, and if they came ashore when he did, or continued their voyage. Perhaps some devout defender of the inerrancy of the Bible will yet consent to be swallowed by a whale for a few days in order to give the world a realistic account of Jonah's remarkable journey.

But although our hero vigorously objected to becoming a calamity howler he took a wonderful interest in his work when he once got into harness. He was only commissioned to conduct a camp-meeting revival in Nineveh and rail against its moral rottenness; but he determined to "bring a corollary rather than want a spirit," so he began to bawl in the streets.

"Yet forty days and Nineveh shall be overthrown."

Such a calamity cry as that, coming from a man whom we have no evidence had taken a bath or changed his shirt since associating with the whale, was enough to frighten a marble caryatid into convulsions. The entire population, from the King on his throne to the wingless buzzard who wrote anonymous communications to the editor of the Nineveh Morning Bazoo, informing him that he was an iridescent ass, donned their sackcloth suits, sat in the ashes and failed to come up to their feed. In those old days a man who filled his hair with hickory ashes and boycotted his barber and his belly, was supposed to be an especially agreeable sight to the good God; hence we can hardly wonder that he promptly repealed the act authorizing the free coinage of calamities. Just what awful punishment would have been inflicted upon the fair city had the people refused to rend their garments and run their noses in the sand, we are left to conjecture. The Lord might have sunk it beneath a sea of bitter waters as he did Sodom, sent the seventeen-year locusts, or saddled it with a mugwump administration. But the God of the Jew seems to have ever been open to conviction. That's where he differed from Grover Cleveland. The Lord eventually pulled his prophet of evil off the perch; but Cleveland strives manfully to fulfill every panic-breeding prediction of his faithful cuckoos.

After the hot wave prognosticator had put out his bulletins he got him out of the city, so as not to slip on his own banana peel, built a jackal a considerable distance from the spot where his curse was to get action, and deliberately sat him down to see the show. He expected nothing less than the utter destruction by a gracious God of the city in which were 60,000 infants—"also much cattle."

The summer climate of Nineveh was almost as sultry as that of St. Louis; and as Jonah lay in his hut with his tongue hanging out the Lord took pity on him and caused a gourd to spring up to comfort him with its shade. There Jonah lay, day after day, we are led to suppose, looking off toward Nineveh, eager to see fire and brimstone descend from heaven on a million happy homes—to inhale the sweet incense of three score thousand helpless babes burned alive! On the morning of the fortieth day we may well suppose that he arose bright and early. This is the day that is to prove him a true prophet and assure him the patronage of princes and potentates, or proclaim him a garrulous old guy with a disordered liver and an ill-balanced head. Either Nineveh or the prophet must be overthrown.

Beyond the Tigris the heralds of the sun are flaming in the sky. Now the great day-god shows his shining disc, lingers a moment as tho' loth to leave Aurora's loving arms, then wheels upward in stately majesty and pours his golden splendors full upon Assyria's mighty capital. The people awake from refreshing slumber, and the streets resound with the same drowsy hum that for a thousand years has been heard in that ancient centre of civilization. The merchant goes about his business, the gude house-wife borrows soap and sad irons of her neighbor and gossips with her over the back fence about the new priest of Baal; the King and his courtiers go forth to hunt the wild boar and the bride bedecks herself for the nuptial rites. Jonah begins to fidget beneath his gourd and glances often upward, wondering if the consignment of blazing brimstone has been side-tracked by another celestial revolution, such as that of which Milton sings. The sun sinks like a globe of gold into the plain far beyond the Zab, and the crescent moon is trying to clasp Love's brilliant star to her concave breast. The ring of the hammer and the shrill cry of the herdsmen are hushed, and from park and garden come peals of mirth and music, the dreamy cadence of dancing feet on polished cedar floors, and the sensuous perfume of dew-bespangled flowers. Pyramus is bending his steps to old Ninus' lonely tomb to meet his lovely Thisbe; in the banquet hall the golden goblet brims with nectarous wine such as Samos never knew, and perfumed lamps cast a ruddy glow on giant warriors and women fair as ever cast in mortal mold. The hour grows late, the music ceases; the hum dies slowly out, and the midnight quiet is broken only by the prayer of an ascetic worshipping the host of heaven, and the yoop of an unhappy married man going home from the primaries in charge of a pair of policemen. Nineveh is going to bed just as tho' no whale had swallowed Jonah—then puked him up when it discovered that he had "a call to preach."

When Jonah learned that the show for which he was acting as press agent had collapsed, he proceeded to file a vigorous kick. That was perfectly natural. No matter how terrible a prophet's predictions may be, be earnestly desires that they come to pass. Jonah had shrieked calamity until his tongue was parched, yet nothing serious had happened. No wonder that he felt that his star was evil—that through no fault of his own a great three-cornered hiatus had been kicked in his political fences. So he went to the Lord, we may fairly infer from the trend of the narrative, and said:

"Look here, you've busted me up in business. I'd a been a hanged sight better off had I taken my stand squarely on the Chicago platform and defended the money of the constitution instead of joining the mugwumps and clamoring for currency contraction."

The Lord said unto Jonah, in substance, tho' probably not in these exact words:

"The calamity clacker, like the cut-worm and the cholera microbe, hath its uses. Here was Nineveh growing careless. It had been prosperous so long under Republican paganism that it was losing sight of the eternal principles of Jeffersonian Democracy. The old town had become deaf to argument and indifferent to political duty; so I stirred you up to grow a crop of anarchical whiskers, an abnormal gall, and spout calamity from the beer-kegs at the corners. You have served my purpose. I will now cut down your gourd, and you must sing small or the sun will shine into and sour you."

POTIPHAR'S WIFE
Story of Joseph Revised

Here was one of Brann's most sensational—and widely circulated—stories. With all the necessary elements of lurid plot, the author stamped it indelibly with his own eccentric imagery.

For more than six-and-thirty centuries the brand of the courtesan has rested on the brow of Potiphar's wife. The religious world persists in regarding her as an abandoned woman who wickedly strove to lead an immaculate he-virgin astray.

The crime of which she stands accused is so unspeakably awful that even after the lapse of ages we cannot refer to the miserable creature without a moan. Compared with her infamous conduct old Lot's dalliance with his young daughters and David's ravishment of Uriah's wife appear but venial faults, or even shine as spotless virtues.

The story of Mrs. Potiphar's unrequited passion may be strictly true; but if so the world has changed most wondrously. It transcends the probable and rests upon such doubtful *ex parte* evidence that a modern court would give her a certificate of good character. It is not in accord with our criminal code to damn a woman on the unsupported deposition of a young dude whom she has had arrested for attempted ravishment. Had Joseph simply filed a general denial and proven previous good character we might suspect the madame of malicious prosecution; but he doth protest too much.

Mrs. Potiphar was doubtless a young and pretty woman. She was the wife of a wealthy and prominent official of Pharaoh's court, and those old fellows were a trifle exacting in their tastes. They sought out the handsomest women of the world to grace their homes, for sensuous love was then the supreme law of wedded life. Joseph was a young Hebrew slave belonging to Mrs. Potiphar's husband, who treated him with exceptional consideration because of his business ability. One day the lad found himself alone with the lady. The latter suddenly turned in a fire alarm, and Jacob's favorite son jogged along Josie in such hot haste that he left his garment behind. Mrs. Potiphar informed those who responded to her signal of distress that the slave had attempted a criminal assault. She is supposed to have repeated the story to her husband when he came home, and the chronicler adds, in a tone of pained surprise, that the old captain's "anger was kindled." Neither Mrs. Potiphar's husband nor her dearest female friends appear to have doubted her version of the affair, which argues that, for a woman who moved in the highest social circles, she enjoyed a reasonably good reputation.

But Joseph had a different tale to tell. He said that the poor lady became desperately enamored of his beauty and day by day assailed his continence, but that he was deaf to her amorous entreaties as Adonis to the dear blandishments of Venus Pandemos. Finally she became so importunate that he was compelled to seek safety in flight. He saved his virtue but lost his vestments. It was a narrow escape, and the poor fel-

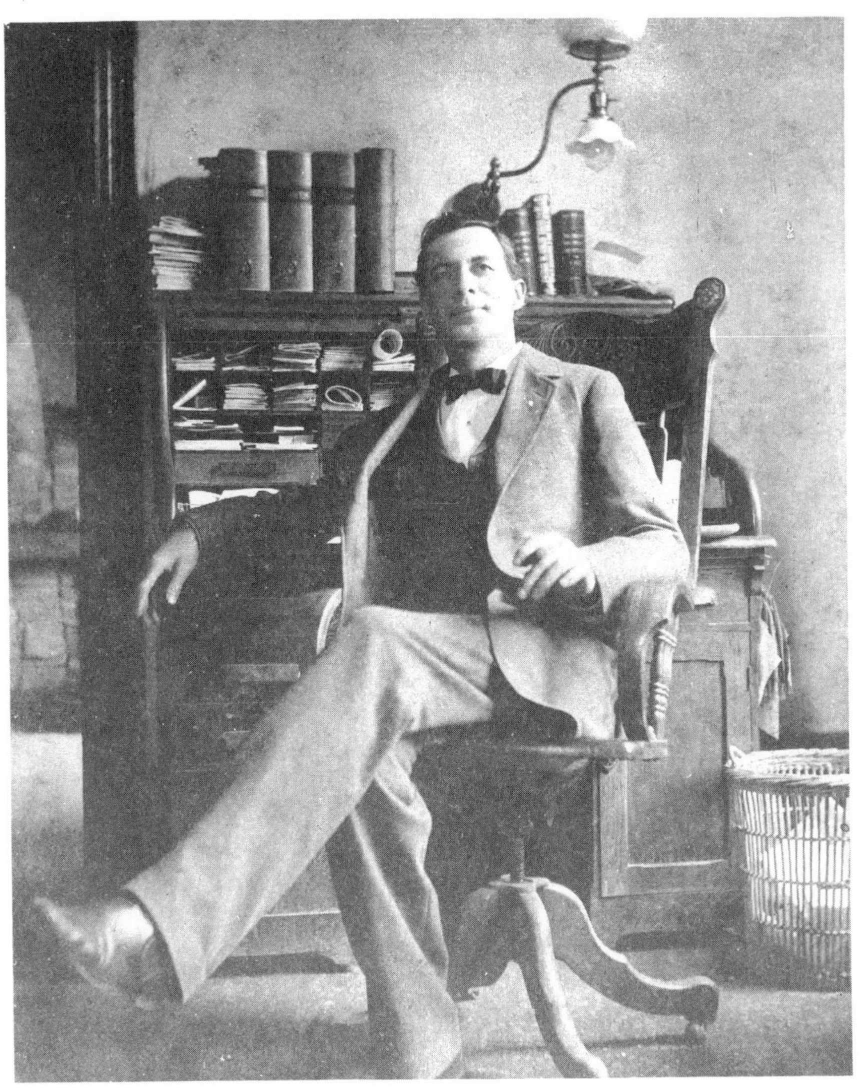

"A fair likeness" of W. C. Brann, at work, and at his zenith, 1895.

Brann's vine-shadowed home at Waco. Here he loved to write, late at night, at his desk in the upper bay window.

PRICE, 10 CENTS. $1.00 A YEAR

Brann's Iconoclast.

VOL. 7. WACO, TEXAS, U. S. A., MARCH, 1897. NO. 2.

PUBLISHED MONTHLY BY W. C. BRANN.

Entered at the Postoffice, Waco, Texas, as second-class matter.

Remit by Bank Draft, P. O. or Express Money Order
All Subscriptions Payable invariably in Advance.
The Iconoclast has no "Exchange" or free list.

OFFICE:—Rooms 32 and 33 Provident Building.

BRADLEY-MARTIN BAL-MASQUE.

"Apres Moi le Deluge!"

MRS. BRADLEY-MARTIN'S sartorial kings and pseudo-queens, her dukes and DuBarrys, princes and Pompadours, have strutted their brief hour upon the mimic stage, disappearing at daybreak like foul night-birds or an unclean dream—have come and gone like the rank eructation of some crapulous Sodom, a malodor from the cloacæ of ancient capitals, a breath blown from the festering lips of half-forgotten harlots, a stench from the sepulchre of centuries devoid of shame. Uncle Sam may now proceed to fumigate himself after his enforced association with royal bummers and brazen bawds; may comb the Bradley-Martin itch bacteria out of his beard and consider, for the ten-thousandth time, the probable result of his strange commingling of royalty-worshipping millionaires and sansculottic mendicants—how best to put a ring in the nose of the golden calf ere it become a Phalaris bull and relegate him to its belly. Countless columns have been written, printed, possibly read, anent the Bradley-Martin ball—all the preachers and teachers, editors and other able idiots pouring forth voluminous opinions. A tidal wave of printer's ink has swept across the continent, churned to atrous foam by hurricanes of lawless gibberish and wild gusts of resounding gab. The empyrean has been ripped and the tympana of the too-patient gods ravished with fulsome commendation and foolish curse, showers of Parthian arrows and wholesale consignments of soft-soap darkening the sun as they hurtled hither and yon through the shrinking atmosphere. A man dropping suddenly in from Mars with a Nicaraguan canal scheme for the consideration of Uncle Sam, would have supposed this simian hubbub and anserine todo meant nothing less than a new epocha for the universe, it being undecided whether it should be auriferous or argentiferous—an age of gold or a cycle of silver. Now that the costly "function" has funked itself into a howling farce, an uncomfortable failure, and the infucated revellers recovered somewhat from royal katzenjammer, we find that the majestic earth has not moved an inch out of its accustomed orbit, that the grass still grows and the cows yet calve—that the law of gravitation remains unrepealed, and Omnipotence continues to bring forth Mazzaroth in his season and guide Arcturus with his sons. Perchance in time the American people may become ashamed of having been thrown into a panic by the painful effort of a pudgy parvenu to outdo even the Vanderbilts in ostentatious vulgarity. Rev. Billy Kersands Rainsford cannot save this country with his mouth, nor can Mrs. Bradley-Martin wreck it with her money. It is entirely too large to be permanently affected by the folly of any one fool. Preacher and parvenu were alike making a grand-stand play. Now that the world has observed them, and not without interest, let us hope that they will subside for a little season.

This Dame DuBarry extravaganza was not without significance to those familiar with history and its penchant for repetition; but was by no means an epoch-maker. It was simply one more festering sore on the syphilitic body social—another unclean maggot industriously wriggling in the malodorous carcass of a canine. It was another evidence that civilization is in a continual flux, flowing now forward, now backward—a brutal confession that the new world aristocracy is oozing at present thro' the Armida-palace or Domdaniel of DuBarrydom. The Bradley-Martins are henceforth entitled to wear their ears interlaced with laurel leaves as sign of superiority in their "set." They won the burro pennant honestly, if not easily, daylight being plainly visible between their foam-crested cruppers and the panting nostrils of the Vanderbilts. They are now monarchs of Rag fair, chief gyasticuti of the boundless realm of Nescience and Noodledom. Mrs. Bradley-Martin has triumphed gloriously, raised herself by her own garters to the vulgar throne of Vanity, the dais of the almighty dollar. She is now Delphic oracle of doodle-bugs and hierophant of the hot stuff. *Viva Regina!* Likewise, rats! Like most of New York's aristocracy, she is of even nobler lineage than Lady Vere de Vere, daughter of an hundred earls, having been sired by a duly registered American sovereign early in the present century. His coat-of-arms was a cooper's adz rampant, a beer-barrel couchant and the motto, "Two heads are better than one." By wearing his neighbors' cast-clothes and feeding his family on cornbread and "sow-belly," he was able to lay the foundation of that fortune which has made his daughter *facile princeps* of New York's patricians. John Jacob Astor, who acted as royal consort to the cooper's regal daughter in the *quadrille d' honneur*, is likewise descended from noble Knights (of Labor) and dames of high degree. He traces his lineage in an unbroken line to that haughty Johann Jakob who came to America in the steerage, wearing a Limburger linsey-woolsey and a pair of wooden shoes. Beginning life in the new world as a rat catcher, he

The front page. Here is a typical copy of the magazine itself, quite inoffensive—at first appearance.

Potiphar's Wife

STORY OF

JOSEPH

REVISED.

BRANN

(Editor of Brann's Iconoclast.)

WACO, TEXAS.

Price, 5 Cents.

WACO, TEXAS:
THE KNIGHT PRINTING CO.,
1898.

Potiphar's Wife—one of Brann's most popular articles re-run in pamphlet form.

Judge G. B. Gerald, Brann's fiery friend and ally.

TO THE PUBLIC:

WACO, Texas, October 21nd, 1897.

In relation to the difficulty which occurred between myself and the editor of the Times-Herald, about a communication left at his office, which he refused to publish and refused to return to me, I have this to say: That it is the universal rule among all editors to return rejected communications, if they are demanded, the writer either furnishing the stamps to carry them through the mails or upon making a personal demand for same; I also assert, that no honorable editor will ever allow the communication that he rejects to willingly pass into the hands of another. When I left the communication at the Times office on Saturday night, I stated emphatically to Doctor Weathered, one of the business partners of the concern—that if it was not published, I wanted it returned to me, and this information was conveyed to the editor. On Monday morning I called for it, and was informed that I could not get it, that it was locked up in the desk of the editor, who was absent. I left a message that I wanted it, and held him responsible for its return to me. It was my property, and I had an unquestioned right to demand it, and I was determined to have it for reasons that were good to me, and which many persons who have since read that communication, will know. It was refused me time and again. Provoked beyond endurance, I at last told him—knowing that I was physically unable to engage in a fisticuff with him, to get his pistol, come out into the street, and we would make it a matter of life or death. He refused to do it. I then left, he followed me up, through the hallway to the stairway, still continuing to talk over the matter, still refusing to give what was unquestionably mine, and at last waited until he got me in a position, where, even if my physical strength had been equal to his, he would have had a great advantage over me, he, by his own acts and by his own conduct provoked me into saying words that he of course justifies himself in striking me. When he delivered the first blow—and I believe he had some foreign substance in his hand—I felt my eye closed from the blood rushing from the gash above my eyebrow; having practically but one hand, then being deprived of one eye, and being nearly double his age, and about one-fourth of his physical strength, I felt perfectly justified in shooting him, and as I staggered back from the blow, I reached for my pistol, intending to shoot him; he caught my hand, and by his superior strength and the disadvantage of my position, prevented me from getting it, and in the struggle the pistol fell and rolled down the stairs; while struggling for the possession of the pistol, he called out "Judge, don't shoot me, I am unarmed;" but the moment he saw that the pistol was beyond my reach, he struck me again, this time with his naked fist, inflicting no damage, which satisfied me that the first blow was aided by some foreign substance in his hand. I threw my crippled arm around his neck, got his thumb in my mouth and proceeded to lacerate it to the best of my ability. In our struggle on the stairway, he got me down, his thumb still in my mouth, and in this position we were when separated. Yet he told the Telephone reporter, in substance, that he knocked me down the stairs and that he supposed my friends picked me up and carried me away, which he knew, and others knew at the time he made it, that it was false. He has made other false statements about this matter that will be demonstrated on my trial. I waited until the excitement of mob violence had quieted down, as it was my duty to do, sent him a message by a friend, inviting him to meet me in a way in which all physical inequalities would be equalized, offering, if he would do so, to apologize for the epithet I had applied to him; yet, unsatisfied with all the advantages he had taken of me, unsatisfied with having forced the difficulty upon me, unsatisfied with having made a false report to the reporter of the Telephone, he refused to meet me, on the ground that he was *no fighting man*, and that there was *no adequate cause for a difficulty*.

These are the facts, and I hereby brand J. W. Harris, editor of the Times-Herald, as a liar, a coward and a cur; as a man who takes every advantage, who lies about difficulties that he has brought about himself, and then, like the craven cur that he is, refuses to meet the man he has wronged on equal terms; but as I understand, forts himself up in his office, with a double-barreled shotgun, hoping that I would go to his office, where he could shoot me down from behind his cowardly breast works without any danger to himself. I had no objection to his using his shotgun, if he had come into the alley-way back of his office, and allowed me to use mine on him. I thus brand him as unworthy of the respect of decent gentlemen, and shall circulate this hand-bill throughout McLennan county, so that in every community where he dares to carry his coward face and currish heart, they may know the proper estimate to put upon him. I am told by some of my friends, that I will be assassinated by this cowardly cur, who will either shoot me from behind some breast works or as I pass along the streets. Assassination is what no man can protect himself from, if the assassin is determined. I pledge my friends, having done my duty to myself and this community, in exposing a liar, a coward and a cur, that I will not hunt him, either in his office or anywhere else, but I have walked the streets of Waco for nearly thirty years without the fear of either brave men or assassins, and I will continue to do so. I have only this to say to my friends, if any cowardly advantage is taken of me and I am assassinated, I leave it to them to see that the cowardly assassin receives his just deserts; also, if any one comes forward, after my assassination and claims that he heard me make threats against J. W. Harris, treat him as an accessory before the fact, to my assassination, for I am not of the threatening kind, and have not made and will not make any threats against him.

G. B. GERALD.

Gerald's yellow handbill, which precipitated his duel with Jim and Bill Harris. They lost their lives, Gerald an arm.

EXTRA.

Waco Daily Telephone.

WACO, TEXAS, FRIDAY NIGHT, APRIL 1, 1898.

ANOTHER STREET DUEL.

Tom E. Davis and W. C. Brann Are the Principals.

BOTH MEN ARE BADLY WOUNDED.

Davis Is Said to Be Fatally Hurt. The Statements of Some of the Witnesses To The Frightful Tragedy.

Shortly after 6 o'clo[illegible] ning a deplorable sh[illegible] tween [illegible]

At this writing the extent and effect [illegible] his wounds are problem[illegible] shooti[illegible]

had i[illegible] in t[illegible] Da[illegible] g[illegible] L[illegible] see[illegible] tell[illegible] the [illegible] Durie[illegible] took B[illegible] to the [illegible]

A nu[illegible] were l[illegible] seem[illegible] ity. [illegible] ver[illegible] of [illegible] bo[illegible]

D[illegible]

si[illegible] su[illegible] D[illegible] a[illegible] le[illegible] m[illegible] a[illegible]

e[illegible] co[illegible] du[illegible] the[illegible] fus[illegible]

LA[illegible] sons a[illegible] shootin[illegible] that Da[illegible] agrees [illegible] Officer S[illegible] the fir[illegible] the l[illegible] let [illegible] w[illegible]

a[illegible] facin[illegible] himsel[illegible]

Brann [illegible] dence [illegible]

The Brann-Davis duel produced a sensational EXTRA.

Brann's body, "laid out" at his home, before the lengthy funeral.

Brann's classic tombstone—a lamp of truth—in Oakwood Cemetery at Waco, Texas.

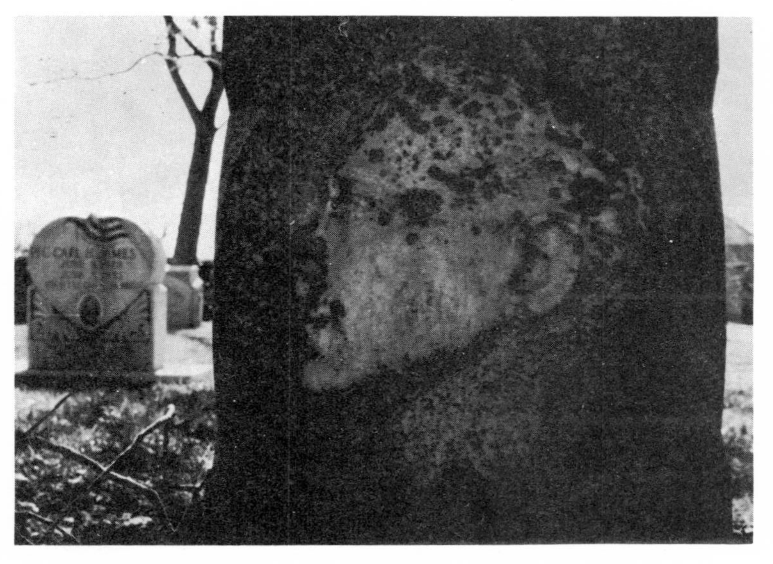

Close-up of the tombstone, showing Brann's bullet-dented temple—the dent a nocturnal later addition.

A Little Journey to the Home of Journalism's Most Tragic and Pathetic Figure

BRANN

THE ICONOCLAST

The Wizard of Words—the Most Positive Force in the Life of His Time

Gall is sublimated audacity, transcendent impudence, immaculate nerve, tripleplated cheek, brass in solid slugs.

Marriage is perhaps the only game of chance ever invented at which it is possible for both players to lose.

Reading is the nurse of culture; reflection the mother of genius.

I confess to a sneaking respect for Satan, for he is pre-eminently a success in his chosen profession.

A newspaper is not the mother but the daughter of public opinion.

On the ancient battlements of San Antonio have floated the banners of six nations, and through her streets for a hundred and fifty years has ebbed & flowed the crimson tide of war.

BRANN, THE ICONOCLAST

Nobody knows so well how to manage a husband as an old maid.

Think of an infant Napoleon nursing a rubber nozzle, of rearing a Brutus on patent baby food, of bringing up a Hannibal by hand!

Character no longer counts for aught unless re-enforced by a bank-account.

The American Drummer is an apostle of civilization, nay, of religion itself—the religion of humanity.

Brann with his iconoclastic torch applied its flame to the purple cloak of hypocrisy and then lashed the burning with such a fury of fiery utterances that the wondering world still clamors for his writings

By ELBERT HUBBARD

A eulogy by Brann's contemporary, Elbert Hubbard.

TEXAS SOCRATES

THE PEOPLE OF WACO HAD REASON ENOUGH TO FEAR HIM, FOR HE PROCLAIMED THE TRUTH

FORTY years ago a job press in the little central Texas town of Waco ground out a flood of smeared, flimsy sheets, the cheap paper covered with the most forceful prose ever to come from an American pen . . . searing sentences and biting ridicule that shocked the staid last decade of the 19th century into startled awareness.

"Never attempt to move an ox team with moral suasion, or to drown the cohorts of the devil with the milk of human kindness," wrote William Cowper Brann, and in the columns of his *Iconoclast* he proceeded to flay the frauds and hypocrites, the shams and social injustices of the day, with such outspoken truth that a contemporary journal accorded him recognition as being "the most dangerous person at an editorial desk in the United States."

Completely self-educated, Brann was master of one of the fullest vocabularies any American ever possessed, and the pages of his *Iconoclast* flow with rich and pungent phrases. At least two of the characteristically American writers, O. Henry and Elbert Hubbard, owe him much of their inspiration and success. And had he not, for his gadfly proclivities, been served by the good Baptist citizenry of Waco with the indigenous revolver in lieu of the hemlock cup, Brann might stand today as a greater name than either.

Stirring indeed is the tragic record of this idealistic, gun-toting, Texas genius, to whom Victoria was "a beery old female," who defended truth with mockery and opposed prohibitionists and the Baptist ministry because they violated his credo of personal liberty. "Would that I had the power to . . . weave of words a whip of scorpions to lash the rascals naked through the world," he cried. Then with unrelenting vigor and courage Brann applied his scourge, scornful of the hatred and threat of death he knew to be the reward. His pen recognized no shackles of conventionality, his cauterizing wit no curb of fear or restraint, and he loosed ironic mockery and scathing ridicule without respect for person or institution.

The pages of the *Iconoclast* provide a panorama of diversified learning and keen understanding that constitutes unquestionable proof of Brann's

A fulsome treatment in Coronet for December, 1938. They still appear.

"An Intellectual
Cocktail."

THE ONLY AMERICAN MAGAZINE
THAT EVER SECURED 100,000
READERS IN A SINGLE YEAR.

Published Monthly at Waco, Texas.

$1 a Year. 10 Cents a Number.

Leading Newsdealers Everywhere.

Full-page advertisement for the *Iconoclast* from *Brann's Annual*, 1895

low must have been dreadfully frightened. Suppose that the she-Tarquin had accomplished her hellish design, and that her victim had died of shame? She would have changed the whole current of the world's history! Old Jacob and his other interesting if less virtuous sons, would have starved to death, and there would have been neither Miracles nor Mosaic Law, Ten Commandments nor Vicarious Atonement. Talmage and other industrious exploiters of intellectual tommyrot, now ladling out saving grace for fat salaries, might be as unctuously mouthing for Mumbo Jumbo, fanning the flies off some sacred bull or bowing the knee to Baal. The Potiphar-Joseph episode deserves the profoundest study. It was an awful crisis in the history of the human race!

How thankful we, who live in these latter days, should be that the female rape fiend has passed into the unreturning erstwhile with the horned unicorn and dreadful hippogriff, the minotaur and other monsters that once affrighted the fearful souls of men—that sensuous sirens do not so assail us and rip our coat-tails off in a foul attempt to wreck our virtue and fill our lives with fierce regret. True, the Rev. Parkhurst doth protest that he was hard beset by beer and beauty unadorned; but he seems to have been seeking the loaded "schooner" and listening for the siren's dizzy song. Had Joseph lived in Texas he could never have persuaded Judge Lynch that the lady and not he should be hanged. The youngster dreamed himself into slavery, and I opine that he dreamed himself into jail. With the internal evidence of the story for a guide, I herewith present, on behalf of Mrs. Potiphar, a revised and reasonable version of the *affaire d'amour*.

Joseph was, the chronicler informs us, young, "a goodly person and well favoured." His Hebraic type of manly beauty and mercurial temperament must have contrasted strangely with Mrs. Potiphar's dark and stolid countrymen. Mistress and slave were much together, the master's duties requiring his presence near his prince. Time hung heavily on the lady's hands and, as an ennui antidote, she embarked on a desperate flirtation with the handsome fellow, for Egypt's dark-eyed daughters dearly love to play fast and loose with the hearts of men. Of course it was very wrong; but youth and beauty will not be strictly bound, the opportunity seemed made for mischief, and Mrs. Potiphar cared little for her lord—a grisly old warrior who treated her as a pretty toy his wealth had purchased, to be petted or put aside at pleasure.

A neglected wife whose charms attract the admiring eyes of men may not depart one step from the straight and narrow path, but her husband's honor stands ever within the pale of danger. Let that husband whose courtship ceased at Hymen's shrine, who is a gallant abroad and a boor at home, keep watch and ward, for homage is sweet even to a wedded woman.

While Potiphar played the petty tyrant and exacted of his wife a blind obedience, Joseph sang to her songs she loved—plaintive tales of tender passion, of enchanted monarchs and maids of matchless beauty. He culled the fairest flowers from the great garden and wove them into garlands to deck her hair, dark as that lingering night which Moses laid upon the Valley of the Nile. He gave her a thousand little attentions so grateful to womankind, and worshipped her, not presumptuously, but with the sacred awe of a simple desert child turning his face to greet the rising sun. They were of the same age,—that age when the heart beats in passionate rebellion against cold precepts, the blood riots in the veins like molten rubies and all life seems made for love, for day dreams golden as the dawn, for sighs and sweet companionship. What wonder that she sometimes left her lord to his heavy slumbers and crept into the cool gardens with the handsome Hebrew boy; that they walked, hand clasped in hand, beneath the tall palms that nodded knowingly, and whispered sweet nothings while the mellow moonlight quivered on the Nile and sad Philomela poured forth her plaintive song like a flood of lover's tears? All day long they were alone together,—those children of the world's youth, when life was strong and moral law was weak. When the summer sun rode high in heaven and sent his burnished shafts straight down into the white streets and swooning gardens; when the great house was closed to shut out the blinding glare and in the court cool fountains cast their grateful spray, what wonder that she bade him sit at her feet and sing the love songs of his native land, wild prototypes of those which Solomon poured from the depths of his sensuous soul to his sweet Rose of Sharon?

> "Behold thou art fair, my love, behold thou art fair;
> Thou hast dove's eyes, thy lips are like a thread of scarlet,
> Thy breasts like young roes that feed among the lilies.
> Set me as a seal upon thy heart, a seal upon thy arm,
> For love is strong as death, jealousy is cruel as the grave."

The song dies out and the languorous stillness is broken only by the splashing of the fountains in the great marble basins and the drowsy hum of a bee among the blossoms. The lad's head has sunk down upon the lady's knee and she is watching the tears trembling on his drooping lashes and wondering, with a little thrill of pain, if he has a sweetheart in his own land, of whom he is so sadly dreaming. She thanks him for the song in a voice low and sweet as the musical ripple of the sacred river among the reeds—she dazzles him with her great Egyptian eyes, those ebon orbs in which ever lurks the sensuous splendor of a summer night's high moon. Her hand strays carelessly among his curls as she punctuates with sighs and tears his oft-told tale of unkind brethren, the gloomy cave, the coat of many colors dipped in blood of the slaughtered kid, the cruel goad of godless Midianite, driving him on and on thro' burning sands and 'neath a blazing sun, far from his tearful mother and mourning sire. How cruel the fates to consign to slavery one born to be a king! His master is a hard man and covetous, but her pleadings shall yet purchase sweet liberty for old Jacob's son, that he may fulfill the high dreams of which he has told her—may answer the midnight messages of Israel's God and triumph over those wicked brethren. Perhaps—who knows?—in his own land he will become a mighty prince and treat with proud Pharaoh on equal terms. Will he remember her, his only friend in a land of foes? Will he think of her when Ammon is o'erthrown and proud Moab pays his tribute? Ah, no! When a crown of jewels blazes on his brow and the sack-cloth of the slave is exchanged for imperial purple, he'll think no more of the lonely little woman by Nilus bank, who prays that Isis will magnify his power, that Osiris will shield him when the Hebrew sword rings on the Hivite spear. He will take to wife some fair cousin of Esau's house, a maid more beauteous far than those who drink the sweet waters of the south. Old Abram's daughters are fair and have dove's eyes; their lips are as threads of scarlet and their breasts like young roes that feed among the lilies. Does not the song say so? But those of Egypt—oh, unhappy Egypt!

"Love is strong as death, jealousy is cruel as the grave."

She bends low and whispers the line upon his lips, while her fragrant breath, beating upon his cheek, sinks into his blood like the jasmine's perfume,—more dangerous to the soul than Aphrodite's kisses or Anacreon's drunken song. By such arts did Cleopatra win the master spirit of the world and make the mailed warrior her doting slave, indifferent alike to honor and to duty, content but to live and love. What wonder that the callow shepherd lad, unskilled in woman's wile, believed that his mistress loved him?—that his heart went out to the handsome coquette in a wild, passionate throb in which all Heaven's angels sang and Hell's demons shrieked!

A beautiful woman! Not the beauty of Greece, on which we gaze as upon some wondrous flower wafted from Elysian Fields, and too ethereal for this gross world; nor that of Rome, with Pallas' snow-cold bosom and retrospective eye; but the sensuous beauty of the far south, that casts a Circean spell upon the souls of men. Her eyes are not dove's eyes that softly shine along the path to Heaven, but wandering fires that light the way to Hell. Her lips are not a thread of scarlet, chaste as childhood and dewy as the dawn, but the deep sullen red of a city swept with flames. Her breasts are not like young roes that feed among the lilies, but ivory hemispheres threaded with purple fire and tinged with sunset's tawny gold. Reverently as though touching divinity's robe, Joseph caresses the wanton curls that stream like an inky storm-cloud over the shapely shoulders—he puts the little hands, heavy with costly gems, back from the tearful face and holds them with a grasp so fierce that the massy rings of beaten gold bruise the tender flesh. Mrs. Potiphar starts up, alarmed by his unwonted boldness—she reads his face with a sweet glance that tells her he is no longer a lad, a pretty boy to be trifled with for the amusement of an idle hour. The Cupid's bow had faded forever from his lip and childhood's innocence from his eye; he has crossed life's Rubicon, has passed at one stride from the Vale of Youth with its trifles and its idle tears, its ignorance of sex and stainless love, to Manhood's rugged mountains, where blazes Ambition's baleful star and the fires of passion ever beat, fiercer than those that sweep Gehenna's sulphurous hills.

Even while her cheek crimsons with anger and her heart flutters with fear, the woman glories in Joseph's guilty love, sweet incense to her vanity, evidence of her peerless beauty's infernal power. She retreats a step as from the brink of an abyss, but farther she cannot fly, for there is a charm in her companion's voice, potent as old in dreams by maids who sleep in Dian's bosom, yet wilder, fiercer than trumpets blown for war. As a sailor drawn to his doom by siren song, or a bird spellbound by some noxious serpent, she advances fearfully and slow until she is swept into his strong arms and held quivering there like a splotch of foam in a swift eddy of the upper Nile. The room swims before her eyes and fills with mocking demons that welcome her to the realm of darkness; the fountains' ripple sounds like roaring thunder, in which she reads the angry warning of Egypt's gods, while beneath the accursed magic of the kisses that burn upon her lips, her blood becomes boiling wine and rushes hissing thro' a heart of vice. The mocking demons turn to angels with Joseph's handsome face and crown her with fragrant flowers: the thret'ning thunders to music sweet as Memnon's matin hymn or accepted lover's sighs, heard 'neath the harvest moon,—she is afloat upon a sapphire sea beneath a sunset sky, the West Wind's musky wing wafting her, whither she neither knows nor cares.

But the angels and the fragrant flowers, the music sweet as lover's sighs and the sapphire sea, the sunset sky and Zephyrus' musky wing are dreams; the blistered lips and poor bruised bosom, the womanly pride humbled in the dust and wifely honor wounded unto death—these alone are real! With an involuntary cry of rage and shame, a cry that is half a prayer and half a curse—a cry that rings and reverberates through the great sleepy house like a maniac's shriek heard at midnight among the tombs—she flings herself sobbing and moaning upon the marble floor. The drowsy slave starts up as from a dream, quivering in every limb like a coward looking upon his death. He tries to raise the groveling victim of his unbridled lust, but she beats him back; he pleads for mercy, but she calls him ungrateful slave, base Hebrew dog and prays all Egypt's gods to curse her conqueror. There's a rush of feet along the hall, there's a clash of weapons in the court, and here and there, and everywhere tearful maids are calling to their mistress, the Sweet One and Beautiful, dear Daughter of the Dawn, Lily of the Nile, while brawny eunuchs, barelimbed and black as Hell's own brood, are vowing dire vengeance even upon the King himself if he has dared to harm her. The culprit glances with haggard face and wildly pleading eyes at the woman, once so imperial in her pride, now cowering a thing accursed, clothed only with her shame and flood of ebon hair. The great sun, that hung in mid-heaven like a disc of burnished brass when she first forgot her duty, descends like a monstrous wheel of blood upon the western desert and thro' the casement pours a ruddy glow over the prostrate figure—a marble Venus blushing rosy red. Joseph casts his coarse garment over his companion as one might clothe the beauteous dead, and turns away, the picture of Despair, the avatar of guilty Fear.

* * *

Love is a dangerous game to play, and oft begun in wanton mischief ends in woeful madness. In the first flush of shame and rage Mrs. Potiphar was eager to punish the slave's presumption, even tho' herself o'erwhelmed in his ruin; but hate, tho' fierce, is a fickle flame in the female heart, and seldom survives a single flood of tears. Already Joseph's handsome face is haunting her—already she is dreaming o'er the happy hours by Nilus' bank, where first he praised her wondrous beauty—beneath the nodding palms when the fireflies blazed and the bulbul poured its song. The love that has lain latent within her bosom, or burned with friendship's unconsuming flame, awakes like smouldering embers fanned by desert winds and fed with camphor wood, enveloping all her world. She longs to leave the loveless life with her sullen lord; to cast from her as things accursed the gaudy robes and glittering gems; to fly with the shepherd lad to the deep cool forests of the far east and dream her life away in some black tent or vine-embowered cot—to take his hand in hers and wander on to the world's extreme verge, listening to the music of his voice. The great house, once her pride, has become a gruesome prison, the jailor a grizzly gorgon who conjured her with the baleful gleam of gold to cast her beauty on Mammon's brutish shrine. She hardens her heart against him and pities herself, as wives are wont to do who have dragged the dear honor of their husbands in the dust—she persuades herself that love has cast radiant glory about her guilt and sanctified her shame. Oh woman, what a paradox thou art! When the descending sun touched the horizon's rim Mrs. Potiphar could have plunged a poisoned dagger through the heart of her paramour and mocked his dying moan; the great globe of fire has not bid the world good night, yet she is weeping because of the bitter words with which she drove him forth.

"Love is strong as death."

She repeats the line again and again. Oh my Israel, is the grave the limit of thy love? Wert thou dead, fair boy, Egypt would enclose thy sacred ashes in a golden urn and wear it ever between her breasts—would make for thee a living sepulchre and thou shouldst sleep in the vale of Love, between the rosy mountains of Desire. Wert thou dead—

The slaves! They will tell their master the wild words she spoke against her love—against his life. She must seal their lips, must command their silence. Too late! Even as she lays her hand on the silver bell the heavy tread of her husband's brass-shod feet is heard in the long hall, ringing upon the bare stone floor in rapid, nervous rhythm, so different from the usual majestic tread of Pharaoh's chief slaughterman. The slaves have already spoken! A faintness as of death falls upon her; but she is a true daughter of false Egypt, and a wiser than Potiphar would find in her face no shadow of the fear that lies heavy on her heart. The game is called and she must play not for name and fame, but for love and life. Her husband confronts her, ferocity incarnate,—the great cord-like veins of the broad, low brow and massive neck knotted and black, his eyes blazing like the orbs of an angry lion seen by the flickering light of a shepherd's fire. He essays to speak, but his tongue is thick, his lips parched as one stricken with the plague, and instead of words there comes through his set teeth a hoarse, hissing sound as of the great rock serpent in its wrath. His glance falls upon Joseph's garment, the gleaming sword leaps from its sheath and he turns to seek the slave. She lays her hand lightly upon his arm, great Egypt's shield, a pillar of living brass; she nestles in the grizzly beard like some bright flower in a weird forest; she kisses the bronzed cheek as Judas did that of our dear Lord and soothes him with pretty truths that are wholly lies.

Joseph is a good boy, but sometimes over-bold. Poor child! Perhaps her beauty charmed away his senses and made him forget his duty. She bade him sing to beguile a tedious hour, and he sang of love and looked at her with such a world of worship in his eyes that she grew angry and upbraided him. Let it pass; for, by the mystic mark of Apis, she frightened the boy out of his foolish fever.

She laughs gleefully, and the gruff old soldier suffers her to take his sword, growling meanwhile that he likes not these alarms—that she has marshalled Egypt's powers to battle with a mirage. The game is won; but guilt will never rest content, and oft reveals itself by much concealment. It is passing strange, she tells him tearfully, that every male who looks upon her, whether grey-headed grand-sire or beardless boy, seems smitten with love's madness. She knows not why 'tis so. If there is in her conduct aught to challenge controversy she prays that he will tell her. The old captain's brow again grows black. He leads her where the fading light falls upon her face, and, looking down into her eyes as tho' searching out the secrets of her soul, bids her mark well his words. The wife who bears herself becomingly never hears the tempter's tone or knows aught of any love but that of her rightful lord. Pure womanhood is a wondrous shield, more potent far than swords. If she has been approached by lawless libertine, he bids her, for the honor of his house, to set a seal upon her lips, instead of bruiting her shame abroad as women are wont to do whose vanity outruns their judgment.

* * *

Potiphar determines to watch his wife. It had never occurred to him that she could possibly go astray; but he has learned from her own confession that she is a flirt, and he knows full well that a married coquette is half a courtesan. Suspecting that Joseph's offense is graver than his wife set forth, he casts him into prison. The inexperienced youth, believing the full extent of his guilt has been blazoned to the world, and frightened beyond his wits by armed men and clank of chains, protests with tears and sighs that he is more sinned against than sinning . It is the old story of Adam improved upon—he not only damns the woman, but denies the apple.

Joseph's posterity, hating Egypt with their whole heart and intent on glorifying Israel and Israel's God, became the only historians of this original scandal in high life; and thus was a youth, probably neither better nor worse than his brethren, raised to the dignity of a demi-god, while a vain young wife is condemned through all the ages to wear a wanton's name. The story probably contains a moral—which wives may look for if they will.

* * *

Of course this account of Mrs. Potiphar's seduction is a fancy sketch; but it is a true pen-picture of what too often happens in this fair land of ours, and may be perused with profit by many a Benedict. The number of unfaithful wives whose sin becomes the public shame is simply appalling; yet no criminal was ever so cautious, so adept in the art of concealment as the woman who values her reputation above her honor. There is no secret a man will guard with such vigilance as his *amours,* no copartner in iniquity he will shield with such fidelity as a paramour. The bandit may turn state's evidence, and the assassin confess beneath the noose; but the *roue* will die protesting that his mistress is pure as the driven snow.

And yet woman is by nature as true to her rightful lord as the needle to the magnetic north,—as faithful to her marriage vows as the stars to their appointed courses. When a wife "goes astray" the chances are as one to infinity that the misstep is her husband's fault. Love is the very life of woman. She can no more exist without it than the vine can climb Heavenward without support,—than it can blossom and bear fruit without the warm kiss of the summer sun. Woman's love is a flame that must find an altar upon which to blaze, a god to glorify; but that sacred fire will not forever burn 'mid fields of snow nor send up incense sweet to an unresponsive idol, even tho' it bear the name of husband. The man who courts the wife as assiduously as he did his sweetheart, makes the same sacrifice to serve her, shows the same appreciation of her efforts to please him, need never fear a rival. He is lord paramount of her heart, and, forsaking all others, she will cleave unto him thro' good and thro' evil, thro' weal and thro' woe, thro' life unto death. But the man who imagines his duty done when he provides food, shelter and fine raiment for the woman he has won; who treats her as if she were a slave who should feel honored in serving him; who vents upon her hapless head the ill-nature he would like to pour into the faces of his fellow-men, but dares not, were wise to heed the advice which Iago gave to the Moor.

Woman is more subtle than her ancient enemy, the serpent, and woe to the man who attempts to tread her beneath his feet! True it is that all women who find the hymenal rites but an unreading of that enchanted spell in which they worshipped devils as demi-gods; between whose eager lips the golden apples of Hesperides prove but Dead Sea fruit; for whom the promised Elysium looms but a parched Sahara, do not seek in forbidden fields to feed their famished hearts; but it is well for the peace of mind of many a husband who neither dotes nor doubts, that black dishonor oft goes hand in hand with blissful ignorance.

The philosophic world rejects the story of Joseph, having long ago learned that he-Dians live only in childish legend and Della-Cruscan poetry. As an ideal it reverses the natural relation of the sexes; as an example it is worse than worthless, for instead of inspiring emulation the young Hebrew's heroic continence only provokes contempt. Men worship at the shrine of Solomon's wisdom, of Moses' perseverance, of David's dauntless courage, but crown the altar of Joseph with asses' ears. Such foolish Munchausentisms give to young girls a false idea of the opposite sex, relax their vigilance and imperil their virtue. From such ridiculous romances, solemnly approved by an owl-like priesthood, sprung that false code—so insulting to womankind—that a wife's honor is not committed to her own keeping, but to the tender care of every man with whom she comes in contact. When a wife goes wrong a hypocritical world rises in well-simulated wrath—which is too often envy—and hurls its anathema maranatha at the head of the "designing villain," as tho' his companion in crime were born without brains and reared without instruction! The "injured husband"—who probably drove his wife to the devil by studied neglect that starved her heart and wounded her vanity—is regarded with contempt if he does not "make a killing" for a crime against the social code which he would himself commit.

I paint man as I find him, not as I would have him. I did not create him, or did his Architect ask my advice; hence it is no fault of mine that his virtue's frail as ocean foam—not mine the blame that while half a god he's all a beast. Mentally and sexually man is a polygamist, and, whatever its moral value may be, monogamy does violence to the law of his being. It is a barrier against which he ever beats like some wild beast of prey against restraining bars. Give him Psyche to wife and Sappho for mistress and he were not content—would swim a river to make mad love to some freckled maid. It is likely that Leander had at home a wife he dearly loved when he lost his life trying to reach fair Hero's bower. That the Lord expects little even of the best of men when subjected to beauty's blandishments is proven by his partiality to various princes and patriarchs who, in matters of gallantry, may be regarded as pace-setters.

I am not the apologist of the godless rake, the defender of the *roue;* but I have small patience with those mawkish purists who persist in measuring men and women by the same standard of morals. We might as well apply the same code to the fierce Malay who runs amuck and to McAllister's fashionable pismires. We might as wisely bring to the same judgment bar Bengal's royal beast, crazed with lust for blood, and Jaques wounded deer, weeping in the purling brook. Each sex and genus must be considered by itself, for each possesses its peculiar virtues and inherent vices. In all nature God intended the male to seek, the female to be sought. These he drives with passion's fiery scourge, those he gently leads by maternal longings, and thus is the Law of Life fulfilled,—the living tide runs ever on from age to age, while divine Modesty preserves her name and habitation in the earth. A man's crown of glory is his courage, a woman's her chastity. While these remain the incense rises ever from Earth's altar to Heaven's eternal throne; but it matters not how pure the man if he be a cringing coward, how brave the woman if she be a brazen bawd. Lucrece as Caesar were infamous, and Caesar as Lucrece were a howling farce.

THE PROHIBITION PLAGUE

Long years before the Volstead Act, the subject of prohibition was controversial and heated. Brann, as ever, took sides and scored heavily for the "antis."

The prohibitionist, like the cut-worm and the financial crank, the red-bug and the itch bacillus, is again abroad in the land. When, in that happier world beyond the skies, we are permitted to praise God without pausing for meals, we will probably learn why he elected to plague this earth with thorns and thistles, pismires and Prohibitionists. McLennan County will put the wet-or-dry interrogatory to herself June 13, at the solicitation of various Meddlesome Matties, and trouble of a similar character is brewing in various neighboring bailiwicks. The Prohibition craze is like la grippe: When you think you have it exterminated and can proceed once more to the enjoyment of life, liberty and the pursuit of happiness, it rears up on its hind legs, sands its hands and takes a new hold. It is harder to eradicate than inherited scrofula, as irrepressible and exasperating as the sullen mutterings of a soft-boiled corn in a skin-tight boot, or the forget-me-not favors of a rabid skunk. I sincerely trust that old McLennan will trample the Prohibition plague so deep into the sub-soil that it will not see the light of the sun again for a century; but it is a forlorn hope, not firmly bottomed on faith. Texas is becoming a veritable hot-bed of sanctificationists, who have conceived the idea that they have been divinely ordained to drag the millenium in by the ears with the aid of secular law. They have concluded that men can be made healthy, wealthy and wise by compelling them to take their liquor out of a jug in the sacred seclusion of the smokehouse, instead of absorbing it from cut glass with seltzer on the side and lunch for lagniappe. They have solemnly decided that it is their duty as Americans and Christians to sit at the muzzle of their fellow citizen and say how he shall load himself. Of course there is nothing in either the American Constitution or the Christian Bible warranting this idea; but men wise in their own conceit, who start in to reform the world, seldom care much for the Constitution of their country or the

Faith of their fathers. The lessons of history are lost upon them, and appealing to logic were like casting pearls before swine. Of course among those who are pilgriming to Prohibition like Peter-the-Hermit's rabble to the Holy Sepulchre, are many honest—and ignorant—men; but they are probably outnumbered by the professional humbugs and unctious hypocrites, back-door sneaks and meddlesome breeders of mischief. The earnest among them are apt to be two-by-four fanatics, as intolerant as Cotton Mather,—men who take it for granted that they've got all the wisdom and goodness of the world grabbed, that beyond their little Rhode Island of intellect are only gibbering idiots and plotting knaves. They are of that class of bigots who boycott their brethren in politics and business for daring to differ with them, and decline to read a book that is not a faithful reflection of their own foolish ideas—lest they learn something. But honest and earnest ignorance, even tho' it resort to tongue-boring and witch-burning, is entitled to some respect. We should reserve our scorn for those sacred mummers who damn the saloon at home and sit up with it all night abroad; who make tearful temperance talks—for a valuable consideration—groan like a sick calf hit with a battering-ram whenever they see a young man come out of a barroom; then sneak up a dirty alley, crawl through the side door of a second-class saloon, call for the cheapest whisky in the shop, run the glass over trying to get the worth o' their money, pour it down at a gulp and scoot in a hurry lest somebody ask 'em to treat; who have a chronic tooth-ache—in the stomach—which nothing but drugstore whisky will relieve; who keep a jug of dollar-a-gallon bug-juice hid under the bed, and sneak to it like a thieving hyena digging up a dead nigger; who rent their property for saloon purposes, then piously "pray the Lord to protect the young from temptation."

The country Prohib. usually votes as he talks, even if he does not always practice what he preaches. He buys his "bitters" by the jug or bottle, and is well aware that whether as makers of "cordials" or corn whisky, the distilleries will continue to run—that the price of grain will not be seriously affected; but his city brother is a trifle fearful that Prohibition will put a kibosh on business, and is not overly anxious to save the country at the cost of a pecuniary sacrifice. Salvation is supposed to be "free," and guardian angels should not be expected to provide their own feathers. Souls are priceless things, of course; but when it comes to purchasing them for Jesus in job lots at the cost of diminished trade, lower rentals and higher taxes, the very elect of the Lord—if they have aught to lose—begin to trim and tergiversate, to patch up a peace between John Barleycorn and their so-called conscience. When a fine amen-corner theory and a stubborn financial condition try to pass each other on a single track the former invariably gets it in the umbilicus, or thereabouts. It is just possible that personal liberty may be preserved to the people of McLennan County by those very Wacoites whose inordinate itch for meddling has precipitated the present vicious assault on the inherent rights of man.

It is not my present purpose to enter into an elaborate discussion of the liquor problem. It is old straw that has been regularly re-threshed ever since the days of good old Noah—whom the Lord tenderly preserved while letting the Prohibitionists drown. A new crop of the cold-waterites has come up—and scientists say that another deluge is almost due. The Prohibition theory may possibly be correct—only egotism can be cock-sure of anything; but it is certainly not in accord with the teachings of the Hebrew Prophets and Christian Apostles. The poesy and philosophy of forty centuries are against it, and it got never a good word from modern science until it had succeeded in placing the wine-cup under the ban—thereby substituting for wholesome stimulants a demoniacal brand of booze. Horace sang to the Samian wine; Luther, the father of the Reformation, declared that the man who loves not wine, woman and song remains a fool all his life long; Washington took his with a little water and sugar, and Cleveland can put down three fingers "straight" without ever batting his eyes. St. Paul advised the brethren not to boycott their stomachs, while Christ changed water into wine at the wedding-feast, when he could just as easily have made mulled alcohol, gingerine, Hostetters Bitters or some other popular Prohibition beverage. It was wine and of the best—perhaps Mumm's Extra Dry, with a white-aproned coon to pull the cork. Were our dear Lord on earth today he would be more liable to transform artesian water into Anheuser-Busch or Kentucky cocktails than to paddle about with the whining Prohibitionists.

The theory that strong drink is an unmixed evil that must be abolished, is not in accord with the genius of this government, which would give to the individual untrammeled liberty in matters concerning only himself. Experience has proven Prohibition a rank failure and the customs of mankind from the very dawn of history brand it a rotten fraud. The people of every age and clime have used stimulants, and we may safely conclude that, despite the Prohibs, they will be employed so long as man exists upon the earth. Banish liquor and man will find a substitute—even if it be opium, morphine or cocaine. It is said that Thor, the great northern god of war, once tried to lift what he supposed was an old woman, but found to his sorrow that it was the mighty serpent which encircles the world. The Prohibs are warring upon what they foolishly imagine to be a frivolous habit of man, but will yet learn that they are running counter to an immutable decree of God—are trying to alter the physical constitution of the human race by means of county elections.

There is not a single plea put forth by the Prohibs that will stand analysis—not one. There is no more reason why we should banish whisky and beer because some are drunkards than that we should banish meat and bread because some are gluttons. The doctors assure us that more people become physical wrecks from over-eating than from over-drinking. Some men commit crimes when under the influence of liquor; but more because of woman or greed for gold. Now if we banish liquor because it encourages crime, we should, to be consistent, send all the wealth and women with it—and, if the ladies don't object, I'll go along. Some men go crazy because of "red-eye," and more because of religion. Shall we, therefore, knock in the heads of our barrels and burn our Bibles? If there were no liquor there would be no drunkards, and if there were no wealth there would be no robbers. If there were no food there would be no gourmands, and if there were no offices there'd be no Jim Crow politicians. If there were no gold there'd be no "reserve fund," and if there were no women there'd be no rape fiends. If there were no water nobody would be drowned, so I move that we abolish that favorite drink of the donkey. The crying need of this country is a gold-cure for the Prohibition craze.

Go ahead gentlemen; make Waco a dry town and give the jug-builders and Dallas dealers a chance. Shut up the decent saloon and inaugurate the disreputable "blind-tiger"—where the most villainous varieties of coffin-paint are passed out by a hidden hand at the same old price. Compel us to import our beer and ice it at home—the bottles will make handy playthings for the babies, and serve to remind them that their fathers are not freemen. Do everything possible to banish trade, raise taxes and drive out of the county self-respecting manly men who propose to remain autocrats of their own internal economy. Let us get rid of those who do not choose to sacrifice their American independence for the sake of a few weak sisters who cannot see a saloon sign without having the simians. Waco will then be such a nice quiet resort for overworked people from Dallas and Fort Worth when they want complete rest, and the grass in our streets will make a charming refuge for the mule-eared rabbit. With the saloon hermetically sealed—at one end at least—we can then turn our attention to forms of baptism, take water in all styles, and live upon one another as cosily and comfortably as a basket of adders, our chief occupation spying about keyholes and acting as informers. And that will just suit a considerable contingent of pious brethren in this good old Baptist stronghold.

"Some were born for great things and some were born for small,
And some it is not recorded why they were born at all."

So sang the poet. But despite the laches of the record, most of us have an idea that we were put here for a purpose, even tho' it be to busy ourselves as sandfleas or red-bugs on the body social—to denounce the foolish doctrine that the "uncrowned kings" of this country must be wired away from the insidious cocktail like so many mangy cayuses from white clover.

IS SUICIDE A SIN?

To the question propounded by the title of this article, the author, with strength and logic, defends the negative position.

A suicidal mania seems to be sweeping over the world despite the prevalent supposition that the Eternal hath fixed his canons 'gainst self slaughter, in defiance of frequent denunciations by the press and pulpit of the *felo de se* as both a criminal and a coward. It is the natural result of an artificial, high-pressure existence, the logical sequence of an age of sham. Everything is leather and prunella, brummagem and pinchbeck. Life is no longer real, no longer earnest, but a mad farce, a Momus masque wherein genius panders to the gross appetites of gilded fools and the world is ruled by the impudence of wealth. All the melody of life is drowned by the wrangling of the money changers, the ape-chatter of ineptitude and the social hullabaloo of fashionable harlots; the roses are trampled ruthlessly into the mire in the mad race for riches, virtue hath become a by-word and honor a reproach. Is it any wonder that so many find the brutish revel unbearable and go forth to meet "the Angel of the Darker Drink?"

Suicide has of late years been made the subject of much false logic and foolish sentiment. The impression seems to be general that all who slay themselves are insane. It were much easier to demonstrate that those who consent to live in such a Bedlam are crack-brained. If all the lunatics suffered to run at large should lay violent hands upon themselves the much-vexed "monetary problem" would give place to blessed silence, sectarian sermons would cease and thousands of busy editors now prizing the world out of its orbit with goose quill for lever and a shirt-tail full of pied type for fulcrum, would don linen ulster, seize palm-leaf fan and join the free excursion to Satan's great winter resort. Unfortunately, the lunatic is in love with life. It is he that stands mouthing and mumbling by the open grave in which wiser men, finding themselves unable to longer endure his company, and unnecessary to Omniscience, have sought the blessed boon of ever-dreamless sleep.

Death is "King of Terrors;" who fears him not fears nothing. The Romans were the bravest of the brave, and never suspected of being a race of lunatics; yet they ran upon their own swords rather than endure the ignominy of slavery. And they were right. "Liberty or Death" was the battle-cry that wreathed old Bunker Hill with flame and burst from the famished lips of our fathers at Valley Forge. Death is the *fidus Achates* of every man who deserves to live. He stands ever, like an angel of mercy, at the elbow of the brave. Those who fear him cannot be free; those who make him their armor-bearer may stand erect in manhood's imperial majesty and defy an adverse world..

The man who snaps the silver cord and leaps to meet the nameless terrors of the great unknown, is never a coward; the slaves of fear are those who linger after the day of their destiny's over and the star of their fate hath declined; who drink the bitter lees of life because lacking the courage to cast away the cup—who live, a curse to themselves, their country and their kind when they could their "quietus make with a bare bodkin." Suicide is a sin only when it injures others. Man's lordship of his own life ends only where the rights of others begin. The most perfect life is not worth the living for itself alone. With

> "The boast of heraldry, the pomp of power
> And all that beauty, all that wealth e'er gave"

there's still more shadow than sunshine, less pleasure than pain. Half a century of sweet companionship with the grandest woman that ever wore the sacred crown of wife and motherhood does not recompense man for the agony that eats out his heart when her cold dead lips respond not to his own. The children that become the very warp and woof of his existence,—his joy by day, his dream by night—what are they but the dread bolts with which Destiny sears his soul as he listens to the surpliced parrot's chant of ashes to ashes and dust to dust! The poet who declared it better to have loved and lost than not to have loved at all, was but a utilitarian, a mere beast of the field, happy if he have a full belly—capable of making "the funeral baked meats furnish forth the wedding feast," of enshrining as empress of his crass soul a woman who had borne children of other men.

With the most of us life at its best is no luxury, but a fierce struggle from the cradle to the grave—days of toil and anxiety, suffering and sin, with here and there a bright oasis redolent with song of birds and the perfume of a thousand flowers, making by contrast the desert seem more drear. We struggle valiantly—for what? To maintain an existence that is a mistake; that our inconsequential names may live for a moment on the foolish lips of fame, then be forever forgotten; that we may accumulate a handful of golden dross to tempt our heirs-at-law to prove us the lunatics that we are. Life is "a battle and a march," at the end of which the worn soldier leaves his body to fertilize the fields and fatten future generations of fools. It was forced upon us without our foreknowledge or consent, and we are under no obligation to endure it longer than we like. We cling to it, not because existence with its cankering cares is better than oblivion, but because superstition hath filled eternity with foolish terrors, peopled it with horned devils and chimerae dire. The existence of man upon the earth may be in accordance with the Almighty's plan for aught I know; but individual life cannot be the result of divine decree, for death comes alike to youth and age. God is not a malicious demon, hence he does not compel woman to endure all the pains of parturition, and awake to life maternal love, only to lay a dead or idiotic babe upon her breast. "Be fruitful and multiply" was the utterance of a barbarian seeking to trace to its source the procreative passion he felt beating in his blood. The survival of the fittest is the law of progressive life, and contravenes the theory that the individual is the result of a "special dispensation." Not being divinely ordained to live, man is privileged to die. Suicide is not a sin against the Author of the Universe, for it is impossible to injure Omnipotence. If the Deity ordained the birth of the suicide he likewise decreed his time and mode of death, and it were as impossible for the creature to avoid the one as to escape the other. God works by general instead of special laws. If the acorn falls upon the rock it perishes; if upon the fruitful soil it becomes a spreading oak. Whether it live or die matters but little, for acorns are many and the genus runs ever on. So with the life of man. If a woman be fruitful she will conceive, and remorseless nature weed from her breed the weaklings—will prove the inconsequence of the individual, the cheapness of human life.

But man must have respect for his obligations—there be those who are not at liberty to shuffle off this mortal coil simply because it hath become distasteful. Filial affection man may owe his parents, gratitude for their kindly care, but naught for having called him into being. If not an accident, it was a conspiracy on their part for which he was in nowise responsible. They did not so much as know whether he would be a boy or a girl, a philosopher or a fool. They knew not whether they were bringing him into the world for honor or for shame. But he may in turn have committed the crime of endowing inert matter with capacity for suffering. In that case it becomes his duty to make the life he has called into being as tolerable as possible. He may have won the affections of a good woman. He has no right to cause her sorrow, to sacrifice the life which hath become a part of her own soul. He must do his duty, must stand at his post like a Roman sentinel tho' the heaven rains fire.

On the other hand, he may be necessary to no one. His existence may be an injury to others. His very presence in the world may be pollution. He may be compelled to choose between the bitter bread of charity and the calm serenity of death, between the slavery of the convict and the freedom of the universe. To such a one the sweetest thought must be that he is privileged to end a useless existence. In the grave he can defy "the oppressor's wrongs, the proud man's contumely." The scourge of poverty, the gaunt fingers of disease and the poisoned shafts of malice affect him not. His heart may be broken, but the hurt is forever healed. His trusted friend may betray him, but the iron does not enter his soul. "Greater than kings, than gods more glad," he mixes with the imperishable elements, "the visible garment of God." The battle is ended, the day of storm and stress is done; all the lawless demons that made his heart their home have been exorcised; ambition's baleful star hath sunk from sight; the fierce tide of passion beats no longer in his blood—"the Lord giveth his beloved sleep."

The privilege of self-destruction adds to the nobility, the sacredness of human life. It places man upon an exalted pedestal from which no adverse fortune, no human power can drag him down unless he wills it so. It makes him absolutely independent, lord of his own life, master of his own fate. It is the freedom of the truly free. Methinks that man can suffer and sacrifice more for others' sake; that he can bear with a braver heart "the slings and arrows of outrageous fortune," feeling that he does so of his own free will—that he is not chained to his habitat of clay like Prometheus to the rock to be prey of vultures.

IS CIVILIZATION A SHAM?

The writer's thought ranges wide and far, in this playful "flight of fancy."

Is civilization a curse? Government a fraud? Religion a lie?

Tell me, thou smiling optimist, boasting thyself "heir of all the Ages, and foremost in the files of Time," where are those multifarious blessings so loudly proclaimed, so sacredly promised in their name? Is it true that in nations most civilized, "best governed," most thoroughly "christianized" the people are happiest, find most of sweetness in life, least of corroding care and that heart-ache and hope-deferred which shrivels the soul like a green leaf swept by fierce Harmattan winds?

Contrast the Europe of today with the Europe of Hengist and Horsa; Alfred, King of Wessex, or Charlemagne, the pride of the Franks. Place all its voluptuous courts and tinseled crowns; its philosophies and philosophisms, parliaments and polemics; its cringing paupers and industrial peons; its wisdom as of the immortal gods and ignorance as of the dull, dumb beasts; its wasteful wealth and woeful want; its magnificence and misery side by side with that earlier Europe, when few were rich, but none feared hunger's maddening pangs; when every man rallied to a chief of his own choosing; when the straightened forehead of the fool feared show itself in the council chamber and only the leonine led the lion-hearted in the forum or the field.

Here in America we boast—with or without reason—that we have the best government ever established by man,—have made the most rapid progress ever witnessed by the world; but are the American people happier, better, truer, braver than before that first hoarse scream of the eagle, as it fell like a many-forked thunderbolt from the troubled sky, bedewing a thousand miles of coast with the blood of brethren? Do the people of this Western World find life sweeter, better worth the living in the last quarter of the Nineteenth century than they did in the first quarter of the Eighteenth? No! in God's great name, no! Our boasted progress is but a mighty agitation of that great ocean of humanity which sends the lighter particles to the top as froth and foam, there to catch the prismatic colors of the sun, while the great mass surges sullen beneath, the only hope of each particular particle that it too may become foam and float to the sunny surface of that dark, troubled sea.

* * *

Progress! Our boasted progress is turning God's great world into a machine; making men but mannikins, who dance, not of their own volition, but because the showman pulls the strings; who work and play, fetch and carry, cut fantastic capers before high Heaven,—even think, speak or blow each other into eternity according to laws which they did not make, cannot alter!

Time was when a man's conscience was his guide, his good sword his court of last resort. Perhaps he was then a "barbarian;" but he was at least a responsible entity, the architect of his own fortunes, the moulder of his own destiny. He relied upon his own judgment, his strong arm and his dauntless heart, for he was in very truth a freeman. Now, after so many centuries of progress, so-called, his individuality is blended in the Society, his responsibility is lost in the State, and for freedom there is bestowed upon him by solemn enactment the inalienable right to do whatsoever a stupid or vicious majesty prescribes—or be hanged! We have now reached that point in our "onward march of Progress" where an "American Sovereign" can own a dog, brew a bucket of beer, shout hallelujah, lose his money on a horse-race, purchase a pound of putty, correct his child, get a shirt laundered, till his field, get married or buried only by and with consent of a majority of his fellow "Sovereigns!" Verily it is truth the Poet sings, that "knowledge comes, but wisdom lingers!" Also that the "individual withers, and the World is more and more,"—is becoming a vast iron-machine in which the soul is stunted, the heart shriveled, and that God-like entity, man, is made but part and parcel of a great engine that is rolling with headlong speed—whither?

* * *

"Equality of man" is now the great World's shibboleth, its dream by night, its prayer by day. Equality of man! Why not equality of all animal, of all vegetable life? Why not make the pismire and the elephant coequal, bring the plain-grass and the Norway pine to the same level, subject to the same laws of expansion, forced to feed on the same nourishment, to struggle onward and upward in the same climate? Equality of man,—and men are born so unequal! Here a pitiful Uriah Heep or other "able editor," ever washing his thin hands with invisible soap in imaginary water; there a Richard Coeur d'Lion fronting the world like a Colossus that may break but never bend. Here an arrant hypocrite whose unctious smile makes the widow lean; there the bluff gentleman whose ear's so sharp attuned to pity's doleful cry that he well nigh starves whilst others fatten on his bounty! Here the fool, there the philosopher:—and we must have equality of man; must make these pigmies and giants all fit the procrustean bed; must stretch here by aid of "public education," must lop off there by means of repressive laws, fostering or retarding the soul of man until this human world is like a great field of stunted, thick-sown wheat, all swayed one way by every passing breeze!

What has our latter-day civilization of which we so loudly boast, our ballot-boxes, constitutions, even our scientific research and improved machinery for the production of wealth, done for the human race? True, it has put a few more rainbows in the froth and foam floating so gaily on the surface of humanity's great ocean; but how deep into that dark sea has our electric light pierced, and how many cold, dead hearts has it caused to beat with true and healthy life?

Pessimism! How easy the cry—and how empty! Is not everyone a pessimist who disapproves *our* plan of saving the world? Was not Gulliver a pessimist in the eyes of the Lagado professors? Was not Patrick Henry a pessimist according to Tory ideas when, with prophetic inspiration, he declared war with the mother country inevitable? John Knox likewise when he cast the foolish trumpery of the priesthood from him, calling it a "pented bredd"? Mahomet when he declared the idols of Araby but impotent fly-traps? Look abroad, thou smiling optimist, and say where are our great men of this Nineteenth century,—the product of our boasted super-civilization. Instead of a Blind Bard of Chios singing a Wondrous Tale of Troy, we have James Whitcomb Rileys; instead of Sapphos we have some halting muses of the Della Crusca School, maundering about imagining themselves "poets of passion;" instead of Demosthenes and Pericles we have Talmages dramatically uttering hopeless inanities, machine-made attorneys roaring like bulls of Bashan, while jurors nod and even the "able editor" betakes him back to his shears and paste-pots in disgust; instead of Alexanders of Macedon and Leonidas the leonine we have Shermans marching to the sea, Emperor Wilhelms parading themselves as "war-lords." We have not since "civilization" took its wondrous leap forward produced a Socrates or a Shakespeare, a Goethe or a Spinoza, a Confucius or a Christ. Here and there a pine forces its head a little way above the weltering, stifling tangle of underbrush; but such a little way that to the historian ten centuries hence looking back over the broad expanse, all will seem a dead, cold, level waste; as tiresome to the eye, as unprofitable to the soul as looking across a parched pampas,—not even the relief of rugged barbaric rocks such as were wont to spring up in the savage north in those old days of which the Sagas sing.

Our present Progress, so-called, is crushing all beauty and sweetness out of life, making of Society—even of the vast Universe—but a machine in which there is neither poetry or wonder, but only power. Neried and Naiad no longer ride the crested wave or haunt the cool-gushing spring; Pan's musical reeds sigh no more in the dark forests while enchanted Dryads dance.

> "The Spirits of the Hills, with all their dewey hair blown back like flame,"

have faded like a forgotten dream before our blazing Nineteenth-century car; the rosy-fingered Hours no longer unlock the purple gateways of the Day for Tithonus' radiant bride; Selene no longer drives Diana's argent chariot beneath the gleaming stars, all happy homes of gods! Gone are the Earth Spirit and the gods of air and ocean; gone are the silent Fates and avenging Furies; sunk in the gloomy Styx is Charon's shadowy bark,—

even the very Autocrat of the Universe is being slowly but surely dragged from his throne by the sacreligious hands of modern Science.

And what do we get in return? A dead machine, *a mechanique celeste,* self-created, self-operative, to the surface of which millions of mites—the offspring of erratic and inexplicable "forces"—are tenaciously clinging; chained together by certain painfully evolved constitutions, "moral motives" generated by Necessity, "progressing"—whither? To equality; to that unhappy state where the fool will be as potent in public affairs as the philosopher,—granting that the latter does not perish from the planet as poets have done; where gold instead of God will be king; where all individual responsibility will be shifted to the broad shoulders of Society, and man, instead of a free moral agent, determining for himself what he should do and doing it, will become an irresponsible child in moral, intellectual and social leading strings,—his whole duty plainly prescribed by vote of majorities or fiat of the King! If it take tailors to make a man, how many humble slaves of foolish law and stale custom will it require to make up one god-like soul?

Were not barbarism, even savagery,—with independence, freedom—better than the condition into which our super-civilization is forcing the mass of mankind? Is not the lot of the Bedouin ranging the desert; of the dusky Indian, living by the chase and breathing God's pure air, enviable when contrasted with that of millions of toilers in so-called civilized lands, slaves in the tread-mill of our great industrial system? What is our "material progress;" "triumphs of Science;" increase of wealth, etc., to the tens of millions of care-worn creatures who do not share therein, but grind, grind, early and late, from youth to old age, until the soul sinks and the body faints with fatigue,—and all for the crudest creature comforts? What to them is the discovery that the world goes around the sun instead of the sun around the world, so long as they know they are going to paupers' graves? What to millions struggling for a crust, badgered and baited by Gehenna-bailiffs, stung by the scorpions of Need and Greed, lashed to frenzy by the fire-whips of ever-present Want, are the subtleties of German metaphysics! What the triumphs of mechanics when every labor-saving device but makes the individual of less and less importance in the great world's economy, circumscribes his sphere of action, makes him more and more dependent upon that Society of which he forms so unimportant a part,—less a man and more a machine!

THE COW

Written in a day when most households kept a milk cow, this essay mirrors Brann at his best in pure humor, barbs aside.

For the enlightenment of city milkmen who never saw a cow, it may be well to state that this more or less useful animal does not resemble a pump in the slightest particular. A cow has four feet, but the subsequent one on the right-hand side is her main reliance. With this foot she can strike a blow that no man of woman born can elude. It resembles a load of drunken chainshot, and searches every cubic yard of atmosphere in a two-acre lot for a victim before it stops. She is also provided with a caudal appendage that ends in a patent fly brush. This she uses to wrap around the neck of the milkmaid to prevent her getting away before she has a chance to kick her health corset off and upset the milk.

A cow will eat anything she can steal, from an ear of corn to a hickory shirt. She will leave a square meal especially ordered for her, and gotten up by imported chef, to fill her measly hide full of straw from a boarding-house bedtick, if she can only steal it. She will work at a crack in a neighbor's barn for six mortal hours, and wear her tongue as thin as a political platform to get an old corn-cob, when she knows she can have a bushel of corn, all shelled, by going home for it. She is a born thief, a natural marauder. Any cow that has been given opportunities for gleaning knowledge can open a gate that fastens with a combination lock, get into a garden, do fifty dollars worth of damage and be six blocks away before the infuriated owner can ram a charge of slugs into a muzzle-loading gun.

The man who has not lived in a small town, where one-half the inhabitants keep cows and expect them to forage their living off the other half, will never fully realize what he has missed unless he starts a daily paper or falls down stairs with the cook stove. When Mrs. B. and I first went into partnership we decided to raise our own garden truck. It is the usual mistake of youngsters. During the long winter evenings they sit by the fire and plan their garden. A 640-acre farm, covered a foot deep with patent fertilizers, mortgages and other modern improvements, would not produce the amount of stuff two moonstruck young amateur gardeners confidently expect to yank from a patch of dirt but little bigger than a postage stamp. Thirty dollars for tools and seeds, ninety-seven dollars worth of labor, and four times that amount of worry and vexation of spirit, results in some forty dollars worth of "garden sass," which is promptly referred to the interior department of the neighbors' cows.

I soon learned that an ordinary gate catch was no bar to the educated cattle in my neighborhood, so I added a bolt. That puzzled them for a night or two, but they soon learned the combination and filled themselves so full of cabbage that cost me two dollars a head to raise that they couldn't get out by way of the gate, and I had to knock down a panel of fence to get rid of them. That evening I brought home a double-barrel shot gun, a log-chain and a padlock that would have baffled a cracksman. I chained up the gate, gave the key to Mrs. B. to lose, loaded the gun half way to the muzzle with tenpenny nails and resolved to hold the fort by main strength. It was a bright moonlight night, and I sat up with a corn-cob pipe and a robust determination to have fresh beef for breakfast if that padlock failed to do its duty.

About 9 o'clock an old brindle cow came browsing up to the front gate. She took a long survey of the house to see if we had all gone to bed. Having satisfied herself on that point, she inserted her horns between the bars of the gate and gave it a gentle shake. She looked at the house again to see if the noise had aroused us. Finding all quiet, she went to work on the bolt, first with her horns and then with her tongue. In ten minutes she had it drawn, and started to come in. She was evidently surprised to find herself still on the outside. Two or three of her companions came up and they held a consultation.

Old Brindle worked at the chain with her horn, but it was no use. They were puzzled. They took a long look at the gate, shook it viciously with their horns, then turned impatiently away, like a man who has run four blocks to a bank, only to find "closed" staring him in the face. Several more cows came up, and when they were shown the new jewelry they acted hurt and proceeded to hold an indignation meeting and pass a vote of censure, after which one old she-pirate broke a horn trying to lift the gate off its hinges. After this mishap they acted so discouraged that I concluded they had given it up; but they hadn't. Old Brindle returned to the attack. She spent half an hour "monkeying" with the gate, and then stopped short and began to study. She had more gall than a ward heeler, more tenacity than an office-seeker, more brains than a boodle alderman. In just ten minutes by the town clock she had the problem solved. With her horn she lifted the chain over the top of the gatepost and walked in, as proud as a boy with a sore toe. I felt like a homicide as I raised the double-barreled gun and pulled both triggers. I felt worse as I crawled out of the cistern, where the perfidious gun had kicked me, and learned that I had missed the whole drove and sent a hatful of slugs and nails into a neighbor's china closet. I broke the gun over Old Brindle's vertebrae and followed up the attack with the garden-fork. After I had chased the entire drove back and forth over the garden a dozen times, and seen what was left of my summer's work inextricably mixed with the subsoil, fallen over the wheelbarrow and ruined a $14 pair of pants, a constable came and arrested me for discharging firearms inside the corporate limits. A young theologian gosling, who has since died of excessive goodness, preferred a charge of cruelty to animals against me, and my neighbor sued for the price of his china and got judgment. Old Brindle died, and the court decided that it was my duty to buy her. I found her meat too tough for eating and her hide too full of garden-fork holes to be available for sole leather.

If the retail butchers are to be believed, the cow is a calf until there is no more room on her horns for rings. She seldom lives to be too old to be carved up with a buzz-saw and a cold-chisel and sold as veal.

After she has passed her time of usefulness in the dairy; when she has forgotten to give four quarts of milk per diem and then kick it all over the dewy-lipped maid who has carefully culled it from the maternal font, the thrifty farmer drives her upon the railway track, wrecks a train with her, and then sues the company for $150 damages. Of course the company kicks worse than ever the cow did, but the farmer secures an intelligent jury of brother agriculturists and the soulless monopoly has to come to taw.

Her consort is less brilliant and more impulsive. He has a surly, unsocial disposition and uncertain temper, but can be very polite when he chooses. He has been known to neglect his regular business to assist an embarrassed man over a rail fence, or entertain a party of picnickers from the city. He has a natural antipathy for red flags, and will cross a forty-acre field to make a mop-rag of one and rub its bearer's nose in the mud—an example that might be advantageously followed by the Chicago authorities.

The calf is one of the most interesting studies in the science of natural history. In its earliest youth it wears long wobbly legs and an expression of angelic innocence; but before it is a week old it knows more than some men who have been honored with high offices and expensive funerals. The calf will eat anything it can swallow, and what it can't get through its neck it will chew and suck the juice. Table cloths, hickory shirts, store pants, lace curtains, socks, in fact the entire range of articles familiar to the laundry, are tidbits to the calf. A calf with any ambition to distinguish himself will leave the maternal udder any time to chew one leg off a new pair of "boughten" pantaloons or absorb the flowing narrative of a "biled" shirt. The calf learns bad habits as readily as an Indian, and the man who did not have a youthful masculine bovine for a partner in his boyish deviltry looks back upon a barren and uneventful youth.

I remember one promising calf that I taught to "bunt" like a william-goat. One day my eldest brother and my parent on my father's side were cleaning out an open well, while the calf and myself lingered near, waiting for a glorious opportunity to merit killing. The old gentleman superintended the work and pulled up in an iron kettle the mud which the son of his youth industriously scraped from the bottom of an eighteen-foot well with much labor and an old tin pan. While he was leaning over the mouth of the well, pulling up a kettle of slush, his suspender buttons groaning and his tailor-made pantaloons strained to the utmost tension, I called the calf's attention to him. The bovine grasped the situation, lowered his head, picked up his heels, emitted a triumphant bellow, shot forward like a baseball reaching for the stomach of an amateur shortstop, and struck the rear elevation of the head of our distinguished house with the solid impact of an hydraulic ram toying with a stone fence. A moment later there was a sound from the bowels of the earth, but it was not the sound of revelry. It resembled an able-bodied cyclone ripping up four miles of plank road and driving it through the pulsating heart of a colored camp-meeting. The calf had forgotten to remember the well, and while my respected sire was chasing the kettle to the bottom, the calf was chasing him. Half a dozen robust neighbors armed with a windlass and a two-inch rope dragged the youthful ox and his unfortunate companions from the pit, and the volunteer fire brigade was sent for to turn the hose on them. I haven't forgotten the sequel to this little story; but it would not possess that lively interest for the great public that it did for me, so I will let it pass.

THE BEAUTIFUL EYES

A riotous roast of one of the country's then most popular poets. Brann disagreed with the popular estimate.

James Whitcomb Riley, the poetical ass with the three-story name, which he invariably inflicts upon the public in full, has broken out again. He grasps his corn-stalk fiddle and twitters:

"Oh, her beautiful eyes! They are as blue as the dew
On the violet's bloom when the morning is new,
And the light of their love is the gleam of the sun
O'er the meadows of spring where the quick shadows run.
As the morn shifts the mists and the clouds from the skies—
So I stand in the dawn of her beautiful eyes."

Beautiful! Slides off slick as grease! But we are pained, Jamesie, absolutely pained to learn that "the light of their love" is intermittent. But perchance you couldn't stand to have the calcium turned on all the time. We learn from the following stanza that even a semi-occasional burst of splendor is too much for you,—causes you to wilt like turnip tops in a green-grocer's window:

"And her beautiful eyes are as mid-day to me,
When the lily-bell bends with the weight of the bee,
And the throat of the thrush is a pulse in the heat,
And the senses are drugged with the subtle and sweet
And delirious breaths of the air's lullabies—
So I swoon in the noon of her beautiful eyes."

Ah, God! A little ice water and a fan, please. Chafe his throbbing temples with a Posey county corncob, and if that doesn't bring him 'round slap a "half-chawed chaw o' nateral leaf" in his left eye! Ah, that fixes him! He revives, he totters to his feet, he smites his breast, he gropes hither and yon in his delirious ecstasy. Once more he speaks, and his words are hoarse with the passion that causes him to wobble in his walk and catch his perfumed breath on the installment plan!

"Oh, her beautiful eyes! They have smitten mine own
As a glory glanced down from the glare of the throne·
And I reel, and I falter and fall as afar
Fell the shepherds that looked on the mythical star,
And yet dazed in the tidings that bade them arise,
As I grope through the night of her beautiful eyes."

Well, dodgast our fool luck, he's squatted again! Stun blind and digging at the roots of the daisies with his fingernails like Romeo pawing up the pave in Friar Laurence's cell! Knocked out and completely done for by a glance from a girl who may have holes in her stockings and a hiatus in her head! Perhaps she was cross-eyed and that tangled him up. We hope the smitten Hoosier will recover the use of both legs and eyes,—that his falling sickness will not become chronic. Perhaps he can persuade his star-eyed charmer to wear green goggles or only squint at him through a piece of smoked glass. He might try splitting a thousand blackjack fence rails as a bracer. By the time he finishes the task he would probably tumble to the fact that he-poets-of-passion are not in demand. Anacreon was the last one that could get the erotic jimjams without also getting guyed. Somebody should take the whole tribe of he-warblers aside and inform them that writing poetry—even good poetry, without any love swoons in it—is devilish poor business for grown-up men. If the poetic muse will persist in haunting a fellow, he is excusable for occasionally breaking into song while he draws a fat bacon rind down the shining blade of his bucksaw; but he should not get into the habit of it. When a sure-enough man can not do anything but warble he needs medical treatment.

LOVE AS AN INTOXICANT

Here was writing which shocked Victorian mores. But the readers loved it, and wore out the flimsy pulp papers handing them around.

Seymour, Texas, Nov. 4, 1897.

Mr. Brann: Will you please answer the following question and thereby settle a dispute in Seymour: Is love intoxicating?

CHAS. E. RUPS.

My correspondent neglects to state whether Seymour is a Prohibition town. Of course if it is and love is listed as an intoxicant, the blind god will be expatriated for the benefit of the makers of Peruna, Hostetter's Bitters and other palate ticklers, popular only at blind tigers. Why the deuce didn't the Seymourites set to work and settle this vexatious problem for themselves? Must I undertake a system of scientific experiments in order to obtain this information for the citizens of Seymour? Suppose that I do so, find that love makes drunk come, and am run in by the patrol wagon while supercharged with the tender passion: don't you see that this would militate against my usefulness as a Baptist minister? How the hell could I explain to my congregation that I was full of love instead of licker? Clearly I cannot afford to offer myself as a sacrifice upon the altar of science. Should I proceed to fall in love just to see if it would go to my head, and should it do so, my Dulcina del Toboso might marry me before I recovered my mental equipoise, and I would awaken to find my liberty a has-been and my night-key *non est.* Of course I shouldn't mind it ever so little, but it would be awfully hard on the lady. I have been baptized just to see if it would soak out any original sin; I've gone up in a balloon and down in a coal mine in the interest of science; I've ridden on the pilot of a locomotive for the sake of the sensation; I've permitted myself to be inoculated with the virus of Christian charity just to see if it would "take;" I've tampered with almost every known intoxicant, from the insidious mescal of the erstwhile Montezumas to the mountain nectar of Eastern Tennessee, but I draw the line at love. Will it intoxicate? Prithee, good sirs, I positively decline to experiment. However, if hearsay evidence be admissible I'm willing to take the stand. To the best of my knowledge and belief love will pick a man up quicker and throw him down harder than even the double-distilled brand of prohibition busthead. Like champagne at 2 g. m., it is good to look upon and pleasant to the palate; but at last it biteth like a serpent and stingeth like an able-bodied bumble-bee in a pair of blue-jean pants. Like alcoholism, love lies in wait for the young and unwary—approaches the victim so insidiously that ere he is aware of danger, he's a gone sucker. The young man goeth forth in the early evening and his patent leathers. His coat-tail pockets bulge with caramels and his one silk handkerchief, perfumed with attar of roses, reposeth with studied negligence in his bosom. He saith unto himself, "I will sip the nectar of the blind deity but I will not become drunken, for verily I know when to ring myself down." He calleth upon the innocent damsel with soft eyes and lips like unto a cleft cherry when purple with its own sweetness, and she singeth unto him with a voice that hath the low sweet melody of an aeolian harp, and squozeth his hand in the gloaming, sigheth just a wee wee sigh that endeth in a blush. And behold it cometh to pass that when the gay young man doth stagger down the doorsteps of her dear father's domicile he knoweth not whether he is hoofing it to Klondyke or riding an erratic mustang into Mexico. He is drunken with the sweetness of it all and glad of it. And she? Oh, she lets him down easy—sends him an engraved invitation to her marriage with some guy with oodles of the long green whom her parent on her mother's side has corraled at the matrimonial bargain counter. Then the young man has a case of what we Chermans call Katzenjammer, and swears an almighty swore never to do so any more. But he does. When a man once contracts the habit of being in love there's no help for him. It is a strange stimulant which acts upon the blood like the oenanthic of old wine, upon the soul like the perfume of jasmine buds. He has felt its mighty spell, more potent than the poppy's juice or the distillation of yellow corn that has waved its golden bannerets on Kentucky's sun-kissed hills—more strangely sweet than music heard at midnight across a moonlit lake or the soul-sensuous dream of the lotus eaters' land. For the spell of the poppy's dreamy drug and the charm of the yellow corn whose spirit breeds dangerous lightnings in the blood, the skill of man has provided a panacea; but "love is strong as death" says David's wisest son. Will love intoxicate? Rather! I should say that Solomon was drunk with love when he wrote the Canticles:

> "Let him kiss me with the kisses of his mouth, for thy love is better than wine."

When a man is drunken, he sees strange varieties of serpents. That's what ailed Adam and Eve. They kept intoxicated with their own primordial sweetness until they got the jimmies and saw a talking snake prancing around the evergreen aisles of Eden with legs like unto a prima donna. At least I suppose the Edenic serpent was built that way, for the Lord cursed it and compelled it to go on its belly all the days of its life. Hence the Lord must have pulled its leg. So to speak, or words to that effect. As an intoxicant love affects one differently from liquor. A man drunk on bourbon wants to trail his coat-tails down the middle of the plank turnpike and advise the natives that he is in town. The man drunk on love yearns to hide away from the busy haunts of men and write poetry for the magazines. The one is sentenced to ten days in the bat-cave and the other to pay some woman's board. Verily the way of the transgressor is hard. Some people manage to worry thro' life without ever becoming drunken on either liquor or love. They marry for money, or to secure housekeepers, and drink pink lemonade and iced buttermilk until there's clabber in their blood. They "like" their mates, but do not love them, and their watery babes grow up and become Baptists. Their affections are to the real article what dengue is to yellow fever. Temperance is a good thing in its way; but the man who is temperate in love is not to be trusted. The true man or woman can no more love moderately than a powder magazine can explode on the installment plan. When the cup once touches their lips it is drained to the very dregs. The chalice is not passed by human hands—the gods give and the gods withhold. Hence it is that we ever find Love's bacchanals beating against the social bars. We laugh at the man who flushed with wine disregards the peace and dignity of the state; but we frown upon the woman who drunk with love sins against our social laws. Man's brewed enchantments may be set aside by acts of human will; but the wine of love creeps like a subtle perfume thro' all the senses whether we will or no, filling the brain with madness, the heart with fire.

THE CURSE OF KISSING

Another brash and breezy treatment of an eternally favored topic.

Every little while some smart Alec scientist mounts the bema to inform a foolish world that kissing is a dangerous pastime; that upon the roseate lips of beauty there ever lurks the bacillus, flourishing skull and cross-bones—veritable flaming swords to keep poor Adam out of his Eden. According to these learned men the fairest maid is loaded to the muzzle with microbes, her kiss a Judas osculation, betraying the sighing swain who dares to browse upon her dewy lips, to well-nigh certain death. In the "lingering sweetness long drawn out" myriads of disease germs are supposed to pass from mouth to mouth in true reciprocity fashion, and, falling upon new and fecund soil, take root and flourish there until the ecstatic fools pass untimely to that bourne where all faces stand so wide ajar—held so by eternal hosannahs—that an attempted kiss were like dropping Hoosac Tunnel into the Mammoth Cave. As the duly ordained guide, philosopher and friend of the scientists—as of the clergy—the Iconoclast feels compelled to file a protest. As the Moor of Venice intimated, there's such a thing as knowing entirely too much. Wisdom that knocks the yum-yum out of life, transforms the fond delights of courtship into an armed neutrality and makes of the sensuous Vale of Cashmere a profitless desert of dead formalities and scientific sanitation, simply to save the life assurance companies paying an occasional premium, should be sealed in some Pandora box or genie-casket and cast into the sea. We cannot blame the bacteria for selecting as roosting place the rose-bud mouths of the daughters of men, any more than we can blame the bees for hovering with drowsy drunken hum about the fragrant flowers; still we were happier when we knew not of their presence—when we could swoop blithely down upon a pair of ruby lips working like a patent clothes wringer in a steam laundry, and extract hyblaean honey in great hunks without Death riding his old white skate athwart our pansy-bed and freezing the genial current of our soul with his Svengali leer. We dislike to quarrel with science, but the tables educed in the currency controversy now epidemic in this unhappy land have made us doubt. Death may lurk in the lover's kiss like a yellow-jacket in a Jersey apple; but that scientist who will go about with his compound microscope, searching into this tutti-frutti of the soul for miniature monsters, is fit for treason, stratagems and spoils. He's not a credible witness and ought to be abolished. He's the Thersites of modern society, and we hope to see some wrathful Achilles take him out behind the smokehouse and talk to him in a tone of voice that would discourage a book agent or a poor relation. We don't believe a word about his little tale of osculatory woe. During a variegated experience of forty years we've never combed any tuberculosis fungi, mump microbes or diphtheritic walking delegates out of our white-horse moustache. Kissing injurious to health, forsooth! Why it's the fount of perennial youth which owl-eyed old Ponce de Leon sought among the savages, instead of filling his sails with sighs of "Gady's soft desiring strain." It's the true Brown-Sequard elixir, which makes the heart of hoary age beat forever like a boy's. It's the heaven-distilled *eau de vie* which causes the young man to forget a combination of tight boot and soft-boiled corn and makes the grisly octogenarian rise up William Riley and neigh like a two-year-old. Disease germs, indeed! Why it's nature's remedy for all the ills that flesh is heir to, *facile princeps* of *ennui* antidotes, infallible cure for that tired feeling. The latest pseudoscientist to discover that the gentle ripple of the kiss is but a dirge, tries to set in the black o'erhanging firmament a bow of promise. He opines that all danger may be avoided if the kissing machines are carefully deodorized before and after using, and recommends that the lips be washed with some chemical compound that will make the most obstinate bacillus sorry he was born. It's a great scheme—but will it work? Will our society belles and beaux now appear equipped, each with a bottle of carbolic acid or a jug of lime water in which to soak their sweetness before effecting that exchange which is no robbery?

or will each parlor be provided with a bowl of bacteria annihilator, which the young man will employ much as the careful cotton planter does Paris green? The plan of disinfection before permitting the spirits to rush together a la Tennyson at the touching of the lips, may work in Boston, perhaps; but out here in the glad, free Southwest, where we still have to catch our hare before we cook it, such an arrangement would clog the wheels of progress and perhaps extinguish Hymen's torch. Imagine the Apostle chasing the beauteous Rebecca Merlindy around a log cabin at some husking bee at the metropolis of Harris County, a swab in one hand and a gourdful of carbonated bayou water in the other! Here in Texas a man must take his kiss with the peeling on or go without. He has enough to do to manage the maid without bothering about the bacteria. And, let scientists with their double-geared microscopes say what they may, that man who gets an opportunity to buss a corn-fed beauty whose breath is sweet as that of a brindle calf fed on clover blooms, need not worry about bacilli. It is a feast fit for gods, so let him fall to, without waiting to have the bloom sponged off his peach on the foolish hypothesis that its component parts are horned hippogriffs, icthyosauria and feathered sea-serpents such as hover in the gloom of a gold-cure joint at 2 g. m. If his heart fails him—if he be not willing to chance the cold and silent tomb for the felicity of browsing for a few fleeting moments in Elysian Fields—let him follow the example of the great and glorious G. Cleveland, Esq., and hire a substitute. There are cases, however, where it would be well to do considerable deodorizing before risking osculation, better still, to let the doubtful sweets remain unplucked, as not worth the labor. This great Yankee nation has fallen into the bad habit of promiscuous kissing—a social rite as stale, flat and every way unprofitable as employing a community toothbrush or an indiscriminate swapping of gum. Whether dangerous disease may be transmitted thereby I know not; but it is death to sentiment and provocative of nausea. A woman should be almost as chary of her lips as of more gracious favors. A sensitive gentleman would so soon accept a bride from Boiler avenue as take to wife a vestal virgin whom every lecherous libertine had "mouthed and mumbled." The practice of "kissing the bride," which still prevails in communities professing not only civilization, but the acme of aestheticism, should be abolished by law under severe pains and penalties. Why a modest woman, who has done nothing worse than marry, should be compelled to kiss a company of men and thereby sample everything from the aroma of sour stomachs to masticated codfish, I cannot imagine. The levite who performs the ceremony usually consecrates the first fruits to the Lord, and what he may chance to leave is gleaned by Tom, Dick and the Devil, until lips that would have tempted angels to assume mortal ills, become foul as the Valley of Hinnom—sweet incense to offer a loving lord! I once attended a church fair in Missouri and there found two local beauties of good family retailing kisses to all comers at two-bits apiece—"for the good of the cause!" "D—n a cause," quoth I, "that must be forwarded by such foul means." I bought $5 worth of the sacred sweetness—then hired an old farmer who enjoyed a bad case of catarrh and had worn his solitary tooth down to the pliocene period chewing plug tobacco and depositing the quotient on his beard, to receive the goods. When half through with the job he struck for a raise of salary! A kiss should be a sacred thing—the child of a love that is deathless. It is the benediction of a mother, the pledge of a sweetheart, the homage of a wife. Promiscuous kissing is a casting of pearls before swine, a brutal prostitution of the noblest and holiest rite ever practiced by the human race. It is a flagrant offense against all that is noble in man and modest in woman; hence let us hope that it is really conducive to disease—that the wage of sin is death.

"THE WOMAN THOU GAVEST ME"

Brann strongly opposed the clamor, then mounting, for female suffrage and other privileges for women. His views on the subject were odd and at times conflicting.

Now that the clarion voice of the reformer is heard in the land, demanding for woman all the rights and privileges enjoyed by the sterner sex, perhaps it would be well to ask the fair client to come into court and establish that "natural equality" so vigorously claimed for her, as well as the fact, if fact it be, that she is being "wronged" and "cruelly oppressed" by the tyrant man.

Is it possible that the dear creature has, for some thousands of years, been robbed of her birthright and relegated to an inferior position in matters mundane simply because her biceps are not so large as those of her big brother, and she has no warlike whiskers?

As her attorneys in the suit to try title to this world's wardship clamor for truth without trimmings, and rest their case upon "principles of justice" untainted by prescription or praemunire, suppose we grant their prayer and proceed to the consideration of their cause unhandicapped by chivalric sentiment.

That the greater intelligence should control the lesser must be conceded. To deny it would be to deny man's right to the life and labor of inferior animals, to question God's authority to govern man or beast. If the experience of several thousand years may be admitted in evidence the subserviency of the minor to the major intelligence is an immutable law of nature. Only equal minds can be accorded equal authority without doing violence to this law.

Is woman man's intellectual peer, entitled to share equally with him the wardship of this world? The simple fact that for thousands of years man has been able to hold her in that "state of subjection' of which her attorneys so bitterly complain, is sufficient answer to this question, is proof positive that he is as much her superior mentally as physically. This sounds unchivalrous, but she will please remember that her attorneys insist that this cause be tried solely upon its merits. Brute force does not rule this world. If it did the lion or the elephant would be creation's lord and the Ethiop and the red Indian drive the Caucasian into the waste places of the earth or reduce him to slavery.

Knowledge is power; brain not brawn is master throughout the world. Had all of Eve's fair daughters been blessed with more than masculine strength their position would have been practically the same. They would have sung lullabies to the little ones, adorned themselves, and dreamed of love and love's conquests while their brothers founded empires, subdued the forces of nature and measured the stars.

And both sexes would have been well content, as they have ever been, despite the protests of self-constituted "reformers" of the order established by the Infinite. Man is creation's lord de fecto and de jure. The immutable laws of nature make his sovereignty both a privilege and a duty. The voice of prophecy proclaims him king; he wears his crown by Divine ordination and right of conquest. Woman was created to be "an helpmeet unto man," not his co-ruler. It matters not whether Genesis be fact or fiction, that such was her destiny she has proven by fulfilling it.

Whatever "rights" and privileges she enjoys must be man's free gift. Man asserts his position; woman can but ask to share the fruits of his victories. These he can divide with her, but he could not if he would, share with her his sovereignty, his power; because he can not endow her with his judgment, his mental vigor, his courage and enterprise. Whether he wills it or not, man must perforce remain the master of the world, God's sole viceregent on this earth.

In very few civilized countries does man manifest much opposition to the enfranchisement of woman. Many favor it heartily, and those who object do so chiefly on the ground that woman does not want it. Let a majority of the women in any state of the American Union ask enfranchisement and it will be accorded them. Let them unite in demanding any particular legislation and it will be enacted. Let them ask any possible thing whatsoever of their husbands and brothers and it will not be denied them.

Woman does not demand the ballot, because her interest centers in her home rather than her country; because she shrinks from responsibility; because she knows that she may safely trust her destiny to those who would die for her.

Paradoxical as it may appear, woman is at once the subject and the sovereign of man, his inferior and superior, mentally and physically. His inferior in strength she is his superior in beauty. Woman is the paragon of physical perfection. It is small wonder that the simple people of bygone days believe that gods and angels became enamored of the daughters of men and left heaven to bask in their sunny smiles. The mental differences of the sexes correlates with the physical. Woman's mind is not so comprehensive, her intellect not so strong as that of man, but it is of finer texture. What it lacks in vigor it gains in subtility. If the mind of man is a Corliss engine, throbbing with resistless strength and energy, that of woman is a Geneva watch, by which the mightier machine is regulated. Occasionally a woman enters the field of masculine endeavor and keeps pace with the strongest, but such cases are rare exceptions. The women who have really taken high rank in art or literature may be counted on the fingers of one hand, and those who have achieved anything remarkable in the field of invention, science or government, upon the fingers of the other.

"It is not good that man should be alone," and it would not be did he, like Cadmus' soldiers, spring full grown from the earth. Man is the brain, woman the heart of the human race. She is the color and fragrance of the flower, the bright bow in the black o'erhanging firmament of life, the sweet chords that make complete the human diapason.

If woman is kept in a "state of subjection," as those who are trying to drag her into court and force her to file a bill of grievances against her companion assert, she is certainly the proudest of earthly subjects. If she is a "slave" she is bound with chains of her own forging and wears them because she wills it. In obeying she rules, in serving she leads captive her captor. Really she is the autocrat of earth, the power behind the throne, the ruler of those who rule.

In all life's battles woman's love is man's chief incentive, his greatest guerdon of victory. For woman he bares his bosom to every peril, braves every danger. It is for her that he subdues the elements and searches out the hidden treasures of earth; for her that he measures the stars and determines the procession of the planets; for her that he fills the world with art and luxury,—for her that he is a creative god, rather than a destructive demon.

Woman is with us but not of us. She is in very truth "but little lower than the angels," and we should not drag her down to our level under pretense of lifting her to greater heights. Give to her every possible advantage; open to her every calling and profession that she cares to enter; accord her all she asks, not grudgingly, but cheerfully; but do not force upon her "rights" she does not want, duties she would shun, and which that beneficent God, who gave her to us to civilize and humanize us, destined for our own strong hands.

TEXAS TOPICS

Here the Iconoclast ignites the opening gun in his extended and ultimately suicidal war against Baylor University.

I note with unfeigned pleasure that, according to claims of Baylor University, it opens the present season with a larger contingent of students, male and female, than ever before. This proves that Texas Baptists are determined to support it at any sacrifice—that they believe it better that their daughters should be exposed to its historic dangers and their sons condemned to grow up in ignorance than that this manufactory of ministers and Magdalenes should be permitted to perish. It is to be devoutly hoped that the recent expose of Baylor's criminal carelessness will have a beneficial effect—that henceforth orphan girls will not be ravished on the premises of its president, and that fewer young lady students will be sent home enciente. The Iconoclast would like to see Baylor University, so called, become an honor to Texas instead of an educational eyesore, would like to hear it spoken of with reverence instead of sneeringly referred to by men about town as something worse than a harem. Probably Baylor has never been so bad as many imagine, that the joint keepers in the Reservation have been mistaken in regarding it as a rival, that the number of female students sent away to conceal their shame has been exaggerated; still I imagine that both its moral and educational advantages are susceptible of considerable improvement.

The Iconoclast desires to see Baylor a veritable pantechnicon of learning—at least a place where the careful student may acquire something really worth remembering—instead of a Dotheboys (and girls') hall, a Squeeritic graft to relieve simple Baptist folk of their hard-earned boodle by befuddling the brains of their bairns with miscalled education. Unfortunately there is more brazen quackery in our sectarian colleges than was ever dreamed of by Cagliostro. The faculty of such institutions is usually composed of superficially educated people who know even less than is contained in the textbooks. As a rule they are employed because they will serve at a beggarly price, but sometimes because their employers are themselves too ignorant to properly pass upon the qualifications of others. You cannot estimate a man's intellect by the length of his purse, by the amount of money he has made and saved; but it is quite safe to judge a man's skill in his vocation by the salary he can command.

I am informed that there has never been a time when the salary paid the president of Baylor University exceeded $2,000 per annum—about half that of a good whisky salesman or advertising solicitor for a second-class newspaper. If such be the salary of the president what must be those of the "professors?" I imagine their salaries run from about $40 a month up to that of a second assistant bookkeeper in a fashionable livery stable. Judging by the salaries which they are compelled to accept, I doubt if there be a member of the Baylorian faculty, including the president, who could obtain the position of principal of any public high school in the state. People cannot impart information which they do not possess; hence it is that the graduates of Baylor have not been really educated, but rather what the erstwhile Mr. Shakespeare would call "clapper-clawed."

There is no reason, however, why the institution should be in the future so intellectually and morally unprofitable as in the past. Change is the order of the universe, and as Baylor cannot very well become worse it must of necessity become better. It will have the unswerving support of the Iconoclast in every earnest effort to place itself upon a higher educational plane, to honestly earn the money it pockets as tuition fees. I am even willing to conduct a night school free of charge during three months in the year for the instruction of its faculty if each member thereof will give bond not to seek a better paying situation elsewhere as soon as he learns something. In any event, when Baylor can send me a valedictorian fresh from its walls who is better informed than the average graduate of our public schools, I'll give it a thousand dollars as evidence of my regard, and half as much annually thereafter to encourage it in the pursuit of common sense.

* * *

I greatly regret that my Baptist brethren, Drs. Hayden and Cranfill, Burleson and Carroll, should have gotten into a spiteful and unchristian snarl over so pitiful a thing as Baylor's $2,000 presidency—that they should give to the world such a flagrant imitation of a lot of cut-throat unregenerates out for the long green. If one-half that Hayden and Cranfill are saying about each other in their respective papers be true—and I presume that it is—then both ought to be in the penitentiary. Brethren, please to remember that ye are posing as guardians of morals, as examples for mankind—as people out of whom the original sin has been soaked in the Baptist pool and whose paps are filled to the bursting point with the milk of human kindness. If you must bite and scratch like a brace of Kilkenny cats, why the hell don't you sneak quietly into the woods and fight it out instead of exhibiting your blatant jackasserie to the simple people of Dallas and McLennan counties and thereby bringing our blessed church into contempt! Gadzooks! if you splenetic-hearted old duffers don't sand your hands and take a fresh grip on your Christian charity I'll resign my position as chief priest of the Baptist church and become a Mormon elder. I'll just be cofferdammed if I propose to remain at the head of a church whose educators, preachers and editors are forever hacking away at each other's goozles with a hand-ax and slinging slime like a lot of colored courtesans.

DALLAS WANTS BAYLOR

Another corrosive volley at the Baptists and Baylor.

I notice in one of the local papers that "Dallas wants Baylor" $50,000 to $75,000 worth. Doubtless I'm a hopeless heretic, but I don't believe a d—n word of it. If anybody thinks that Dallas will put up $25,000 cash to secure the removal thither of Baylor he can find a man about these premises who will make him a 2-to-1 game that his believer is 'way off its base. Dallas doesn't want Baylor even a little bit. There isn't a town in this world that wants it except Waco. It is simply another Frankenstein monster that has destroyed its architect.

Baylor spends no money here worth mentioning. Its students are chiefly forks-of-the-creek yaps who curry horses or run errands for their board and wear the same undershirt the year 'round. They take but two baths during their life-time—one when they are born, the other when they are baptized. The institution is worth less than nothing to any town. It is what Ingersoll would call a storm-centre of misinformation. It is the Alma Mater of mob violence. It is a chronic breeder of bigotry and bile.

As a small Waco property owner, I will give it $1000 any time to move to Dallas, and double that amount if it will go to Honolulu or hell. There is no bitterness in this, no desire to offend; it is simply a business proposition by a business man who realizes that Baylor is a disgrace to the community, is playing Old Man of the Sea to Waco's Sinbad. The town could well afford to give it $100,000 to "pull its freight."

ANTONIA TEIXEIRA

In this caustic diatribe against Baylor, Brann unloosed the full force of his invective. The incident involved was tragedy, but Brann fanned it into an inferno—while a multitude applauded.

The Iconoclast is not in the habit of commenting on particular social ulcers and special sectarian scandals. It prefers to deal with broad principle rather than individual offenders. To even catalogue the sexual crimes of professing Christians and people of social pre-eminence—to turn the calcium for even a moment into all the gruesome closets of "respectability" and upon every sectarian cesspool redolent with "the odor of sanctity"—would consume the space of such a periodical, while proving about as profitable as pointing out each festering pustule on the person of a Hot Springs habitue trailing blindly in the wake of the Pandemian Venus; but once or twice in a decade a case arises so horrible in conception, so iniquitous in outline, so damnable in detail that it were impossible to altogether ignore it. Such a case has just come to light, involving Baylor University, that Bulwark of the Baptist Church. I fain would pass it by, knowing as I do that a criticism, however dispassionate and just, will be misconstrued by those good Baptist brethren who tried to muzzle me while ex-Priest Slattery foully defamed me, and whose religion teaches them that "with what judgment ye judge ye shall be judged; and with what measure ye mete it shall be measured to you again." But on this point they have naught to fear. Had they, for every sneaking lie they have told about me, spawned a thousand; and had "Brother" Slattery, in the fullness of his Baptist Charity, branded me as a horse-thief and proved it, I could not, tho' vindictive as Thersites and gifted with the vocabulary of a Carlyle, do even and exact justice to the case of Antonia Teixeira. Crimes similar in some respects have been committed in White Chapel and on Boiler avenue; but, to borrow from Macaulay, "When we put everything together—sensuality, poltroonery, baseness, effrontery, mendacity, barbarity—the result is something which in a novel we should condemn as caricature, and to which, we venture to say, no parallel can be found in history." It is a case wherein "the qualities which are the proper objects of hatred, and the qualities which are the proper objects of contempt," preserve an exquisite and absolute harmony. Three times I have essayed to write of this enormous iniquity, this subter-brutish crime against the chastity of childhood, and thrice I have laid down my pencil in despair. As there is a depth of the sea to which the plummet will not descend, so are there depths of human depravity which mind cannot measure. Language hath its limits, and even a Dante could only liken the horrors of hell to earthly symbols. It were as impossible to describe in print the case of Antonia Teixeira as to etch a discord or paint a stench. Before justice can be done to such a subject a new language must be invented—a language whose words are coals of juniper-wood, whose sentences are woven with a warp of aspics' fangs and a woof of fire.

We all remember the coming to Texas of Antonia Teixeira, the dove-eyed heteroscian, and the brass-band display made of the modest little thing by the Baptist brethren, whose long years of missionary labor in Brazil had snatched her from the Papal power—a veritable brand from the burning. A tardy consent had been wrung from her widowed mother that Antonia should be brought to Texas. The child was to be given five years' schooling, then returned to her native land to point out to her benighted Catholic countrymen the water route to the Celestial City. Relying upon this promise, the simple Brazilian woman consigned her little wild-flower to the bosom of the Baptist church. Five years! What an eternity! How they would miss her at home—how they would count the days until she returned to them, a cultured lady, as wise even as the strange priests who spoke the English tongue! It must be for the best, she thought; so the poor woman crushed her heart in the name of Christ and took up her cross. And Antonia? How bright the world before her! To be educated, and useful and honored both in this world and the world to come, instead of an ignorant little beggar about the streets of Bahia. Bearded men prayed over her and sentimental women wept to know that she was saved—saved from the purgatorium of Popery! And then she was "consecrated" and began her studies at Baylor, the duly ordained "ward of the Baptist church." Not yet 13 years old, and such honors paid her—what might she not expect in the years to be? How the poor little heart must have swelled with gratitude to the good Baptist brethren, and how she must have loved everything, animate and inanimate, that the good God had made. But ere long she found herself in Dr. Burleson's kitchen instead of the classroom. Instead of digging Greek roots she was studying the esculent tuber. Instead of being prepared for missionary work, this "ward of the Baptist church" was learning the duties of the scullion—and Dr. Burleson has informed the world through the public prints that as a servant she was not worth her board and clothes. But then she was not brought hither to sling pots, but to prepare for the saving of souls. Surely the blessed Baptist church will provide its little "ward" with board and clothes. Perhaps the poor child thought that scrubbing floors and playing under-servant was part of a liberal education, for she made no complaint to her self-constituted guardians. After some three years of the kitchen curriculum she was examined in the office of a secular official and it was there found that she had not made much progress toward effective missionary work. She had heard something of the Protestant faith and salvation by water, but did not understand it. And in two years more her "education" would be complete—the promise made to her mother redeemed! But suddenly it was discovered that the "ward of the Baptist church" was about to give birth to a babe. Day by day this mournful fact became more in evidence, and finally her dish-rag and scrub-broom studies were suspended because of a press of more important business. She was sneaked off to a private house and nothing said about her condition to the secular authorities—no steps taken to bring the destroyer of this child in short dresses to justice. But the meddlesome officials concluded to look after the "ward of the Baptist church" a little, and the poor child told them, reluctantly enough, how she had been dragged from her culinary classroom, drugged and three times criminally assaulted—how she complained, "but nothing was done about it." A medical examination demonstrated conclusively that she had been the victim of foul play. What did the aged president of Baylor, that sanctorum of the Baptist church, do about it? Did he assist in bringing to justice the man who had dared invade the sanctity of his household and despoil the duly ordained "ward of the Baptist church?" Not exactly. He rushed into print with a statement to the effect that the child was a thief and "crazy after the boys"—that he had "prayed and wept over her" without avail. Are prayers and tears the only safeguards thrown around fourteen-year-old girls at Baylor? They do those things differently in Convent schools—supplement prayers and tears with a watchful care that makes illicit intercourse practically impossible. No matter how "crazy after the boys' a girl in short dresses may be, she is not permitted to go headlong to the devil—to be torn to pieces and impregnated by some lousy and lecherous male mastodon. Dr. Burleson considered the idea that Antonia had been ravished as ridiculous, yet the doctors declare it one of the most damnable cases of outrage and laceration within their knowledge—and in matters of this kind a wicked and perverse generation is more likely to believe doctors of medicine than doctors of divinity. The students at Baylor declare that instead of being "crazy after the boys" Antonia was particularly modest and womanly. But had she been the brazen little thing which Dr. Burleson hastened to brand her, what were his duties in the premises: to guard her with especial care, or give the "boys" an opportunity to work their will, then turn her out with a Baptist bastard at the half-developed breast? Enciente at 14, among strangers who had promised her mother that no harm should befall her. A mother while still in short dresses, and branded in the public prints as a bawd by people who worship One who forgave Mary Magdalen! We might have expected the very devils in hell to weep for the pity of it, but "Christian charity" had not yet reached its *ultima thule.* Another Baptist reverend had to have his say. He was somewhat interested in the matter, his brother having been named by Antonia as her ravisher. This reverend gentleman tried to make it appear that the father of her unborn child was a negro servant and her accepted paramour. Had this been true, what an "ad" for Baylor University—that fourteen-year-old girls committed to its care conceived children by coons! Dr. Burleson's pious son-in-law, and Antonia replied to this insult added to injury by putting a white child in evidence—a child with the pale blue eye and wooden face characteristic of those who thus defamed her. When the girl's condition became known the men about town—"publicans and sinners" such as Christ sat with, preferring their society to that of the pharisees—raised a handsome purse to provide for her and the young Baptist she was about to bring into the world, while those who should have guarded and protected her were resorting to every artifice human ingenuity could devise to blacken her name, to forestall pity, prevent charity and make an impartial trial of the case impossible. While men who never professed religion, who never expect to wear feathers and fly thro' Elysian fields, could not talk to each other about the case without crying, those wearing God's livery were eager to trample her down to the deepest hell to preserve the credit of their denomination. If there is anything on earth calculated to make a public prostitute of an unfortunate girl it is the treatment the Baptist brethren have accorded Antonia Teixeira.

At this writing (June 27) the preliminary trial awaits the convalescence of the child mother. I would not pre-judge the case. I know not who is the guilty man; but I do know that this child was brought from her far-away home by men who promised to protect her and transform her into a cultured and useful woman, and who so far neglected their duty that she was debauched at Baylor University and her young life forever blighted. Better a thousand times that she should have remained in Brazil to say her pater nosters in the Portuguese tongue; better that she should have wedded a water-carrier in her native land and reared up sturdy sons and daughters to the Church of Rome, than to have been transported to Texas to breed illegitimate Baptists. I do know that at the very time "Brother" Slattery was writing us against the awful dangers of convent schools—and impeaching the chastity of the Catholic sisterhoods—and the Waco Baptist were crying "awmen"—this 14-year-old girl was growing great with child at Baylor University! I do know that while we were being assured that among all the nuns there was not one educated woman—not one competent to superintend the education of a child—a girl was completing her third year in the greatest educational institute the Baptists of Texas can boast, and in all that time she had learned but little, and that little she could have acquired almost as well in "Hell's Half-Acre.' I do know that Antonia is not the first young girl to be sent from Baylor in disgrace—that she is not the first to complain of criminal assault within its sanctified walls. I do know that should a girl meet with a mishap at a convent school the Catholic priests would not turn against her and insult her family and her race by trying to fasten the fatherhood of her unborn babe upon a negro servant. I do know that instead of trying to drive the unfortunate girl to the "Reservation" with cowardly calumnies, they would draw around her the sacred circle of the Church of Rome, and if there remained within her heart one spark of noble womanhood it would be fanned by the white wings of love and charity into ethereal flame. I do know that if Antonia Teixeira was a Catholic instead of a half-baked Baptist, every man within that church would be her brother, every woman her sister,—that every church bearing the cross would be her house of refuge. I do know that so far as Baylor University is concerned the day of its destiny is over and the star of its fate hath declined; that the brutal treatment the Brazilian child received at its hands will pass into history as the colossal crime of the age, and that generations yet to be will couple its name with curses deep as those which Roman matrons heaped on the head of Sextus Tarquinius—"he that wrought the deed of shame."

BAYLOR'S REJOINDER

[From the September, 1895, Iconoclast]

Pressing his advantage, Brann kept Baylor on the defensive, and, like a smart attorney, twisted their own pronouncements against them.

The Iconoclast must beg the forbearance of its readers for again referring to the pitiful case of Antonia Teixeira, the duly ordained "ward of the Baptist church," who, while being educated at Baylor University for missionary work in Brazil, became the mother of an illegitimate babe. She was not the first young girl to get at Baylor more "education" than she could comfortably carry; but, owing to careful concealment "for the sake of Christ," hers is the only mishap that became a *cause celebre,* and therefore legitimately within the pale of journalistic criticism.

The Iconoclast did not find fault with Baylor for the child's misfortune, fully realizing that accidents will occasionally occur even in the best regulated sectarian seminaries; but it did criticize Dr. Burleson for trying to shield that institution by branding as a willful bawd the fatherless little foreigner committed to its care. It called attention to the fact that, instead of striving to bring to justice the lecherous scoundrel who dared invade the sacred precincts of Baylor and debauch a child, Dr. Burleson employed all his energy and influence to protect the man accused of the crime—to so prejudice the public mind that an impartial trial of the case would be impossible. It pointed out, with all the courtesy at its command, that a kitchen was hardly the proper place in which to educate "the ward of the Baptist church" and fit her for the conversion of her Catholic countrymen. It insisted that a child of fourteen, far removed from a mother's kindly care, a stranger in a strange land—and duly dedicated to the cause of Christ—should be tenderly guarded by those who have willingly assumed the duty of teachers and the responsibilities of parents; that if, despite those safeguards which humanity suggests, she is despoiled, with or without her consent, heaven and earth should be moved to land the godless libertine within the clutches of the law. It argued that had Antonia been really so bad as Dr. Burleson painted her, it was his duty as a Christian gentleman to shield her, as far as possible, from public shame, and attempt by every legitimate means to effect her reformation, instead of denouncing her in public and turning her adrift to go headlong to the devil. Mary Magdalen was a professional prostitute, an experienced woman of the world; yet the Son of God freely forgave her—never once thought of catalogueing her crimes in the public prints. Cannot his professed disciples do as much for an ignorant child in short dresses?

Baylor has made no reply to the criticisms of the Iconoclast; but it has tried to. After mature deliberation by its factotums and friends, it was decided to call the turn on the editor of the Iconoclast—to make him crawl into some obscure cavity or get off the earth. Rev. S. L. Morris, Dr. Burleson's pious son-in-law, was deputed to enact the role of Nemesis and make the presumptious critic hard to catch. And all this time the poor miserable worm of the dust wotted not that he was marked for destruction—had no idea that an avenging angel was camping on his trail with the stylus of Cato in one hand and the faber of Junius in the other—that the polemical Popocatapetl of the Rev. S. L. Morris was about to erupt?

How did this intellectual Hercules proceed to the extermination of the iconoclastic Hydra? What was his defense of Dr. Burleson? What his reply to the alleged calumnious utterances of the Iconoclast? Did he attempt a logical defense of the brutal treatment by Baylor of the little stranger who was debauched within its gates? Did he explain why, to shield his brother, he, in the plentitude of his Christian charity, attempted to bulldoze Antonia into a confession that a coon was the father of her unborn babe? Did he give good and sufficient reasons why the unfortunate girl was driven from Baylor's inhospitable doors,—to die on a dunghill if none proved more compassionate than himself and Dr. Burleson, both of whom wear the livery of a Lord who was the incarnation of Charity, the avatar of Love? Did he explain why an attempt was made to "fix" the local papers and thereby prevent the shameful affair reaching the general public?—why the authorities did not report the case to the police and assist them to capture and convict the criminal? Did he state how it happened that "the ward of the Baptist Church" was slinging hash as an under-servant in Dr. Burleson's kitchen, instead of acquiring that education promised when she was torn away from her mother's bosom in faraway Brazil by officious Baptists?

Not exactly. The Rev. S. L. Morris knew a trick worth two of that. Being a consistent Christian, he scorned to waste his controversial powers in the barren field of logic and the realm of common-place fact. He has his own peculiar method of confuting criticism—a method which stamps him as a Napoleon of polemics. He fished about in that foul literary cess-pool yclept the San Antonio *Light,* and there found an article reflecting on the character of the editor of the Iconoclast. It was the same which ex-Priest Slattery—another "Baptist minister in good standing"—attempted to exploit at a stag-party of pietists who had put up 50 cents each to hear that the Roman Catholic sisterhoods are composed chiefly of courtesans. This article the Rev. S. L. Morris requested the Waco *News* to reproduce—as Baylor's reply to Brann! He was told that if the article appeared he would have to father it; but this the careful Christian declined to do. He desired to strike in the dark, to stab the critic of Baylor in the back; and not being permitted to do so, this literary warrior bold declined the controversy and "Baylor stood on its dignity!" This "dignity" would have appeared to better advantage had not the president of Baylor and a number of his coadjutors tried, by threats of prosecution, to prevent newsboys selling the Iconoclast—while Dr. Burleson's son, a prominent merchant, was passing the paper over his counters and raking in the cash!

Just what the opinions anent the "Apostle" held by an obscure newspaper—published for a clientele of coons—may have to do with the brutal debauchment of Antonia Teixeira at Baylor University, I am unable to understand; still I regret that the *News* declined to republish the article in question, and at the same time relieve the Rev. S. L. Morris of all responsibility. It would have afforded several pious souls considerable satisfaction and been an excellent advertisement for the Iconoclast. The enmity of a coon-courting sheet should be a powerful recommendation to every white man in America. Furthermore, it would have saved Bro. Morris the trouble of carrying Baylor's crushing "answer" about in his pocket and surreptitiously showing it to those kind Christian people who dote on calumny. It would have enabled him to devote more time to prayer—and leg-pulling.

The attempted defense of Baylor by Burleson's son-in-law is eminently worthy that institution, and tracks the line mapped out in its dealings with Antonia Teixeira. The offense and defense preserve the unities—fit each other like the upper and lower jaws of a wild beast. With the first as premise the last is the logical sequence, for brutality and cowardice are correlatives—crime and calumny are boon companions. If, at the age of fourteen, the Portuguese girl was fond of young gentlemen, it follows, as a matter of course—according to the logic of this great institution of learning—that she was a child of the devil and devoted to destruction. That she cared for the society of the opposite sex proved hers an aggravated case of total depravity hitherto unheard of in the annals of young womanhood, and relieved Baylor of responsibility. If in all the great universe of God there can be found some Jim Crow newspaper to speak ill of the editor of the Iconoclast, his right to plead the cause of injured innocence is thereby revoked. If he once gets the worst of it in a personal difficulty with a man double his weight, that fact amply demonstrates that Baylor did its entire duty by Antonia Texeira and is a proper guardian for innocent girls.

Now a word anent the story behind which this great educational institute has taken refuge from candid criticism. I have not hitherto dignified it by a line of type, simply because I cared absolutely nothing about it, and had no inclination to turn the iconoclastic batteries loose on a bad smell. I am ever ready to break a lance with the lords of literature, but studiously avoid controversies with intellectual lice. Samson might bestride a lion, but he would steer clear of a skunk. But since the article in question has become the Achillean shield of that professional apostate, ex-Priest Slattery, and Baylor's excuse for the debauchment of babes, it is my duty to demolish it. My private character, *per se,* is of no consequence to the public. I have no objection to poisonous little spiders toiling early and late to weave for me a robe of infamy; but when professional humbugs and brutal hypocrites begin to build their nests in the tail of the garment it has got to go.

While I was editor of the San Antonio *Express* a resident of that city publicly denounced one trusted employe of the paper as a falsifier, another as a liar, ingrate and ex-convict. Believing that a paper that will not stand by the men who make it as a disgrace to journalism, I proceeded to "roast" the complainant. I expected trouble, for he was a powerful (tho' one-armed) Hercules who had beaten up several larger men than myself on less provocation. Instead of coming to me, however, he went to the proprietor of the paper, who proceeded to print an abject apology, not as coming from himself, but from the "editor." Perhaps he had no intention of doing me an injustice—was simply so badly scared that he didn't know who the editor was. I promptly resigned, and as he refused to publish a card to the effect that I was no longer editor of the *Express* and not responsible for the apology, I carried it to the *Light.* I was there suddenly assaulted by the man I had criticised and got the worst of the fisticuff. While I was *hors du combat* he took an oath that if I did not print a retraction of the article next morning he would blow my brains out. Instead of printing a retraction I slipped a six-shooter into the bust of my trousers and awaited the obsequies. Friends of my assailant came to me and represented that he desired no further trouble and withdrew his threat. I had begun to suspect that I had criticised him for telling the even and exact truth,—that I could scarce afford a shooting-match on behalf of grown men who remained in the employ of a paper that had apologizel for resenting the charge that they were a couple of lying curs. So the matter was settled. My article stood unretracted, his blow went unavenged. I had used the *Light* for my sport—much as a mischievous monkey might a Mexican toad. I had invaded its sanctum but a few days before with the avowed intention of trimming the ears of its editor, but found him conveniently absent. He had been soundly kicked by one employe of the *Express* (Dickinson) and his city editor chased down Commerce Street and cuffed by another (Hollub). Naturally the *Light* was filled to the bursting point with bile, and proceded to "play for even" by printing the article which Baylor now offers in extenuation of its cruel treatment of Antonia Teixeira, and to send lying specials to other papers. I cared so little for what the *Light* might say that I did not read the article until it became the bulwark of Baylor more than a year afterwards, althought I knew it was being carried about in the pockets of ministerial mountebanks like Sid Williams and Sam Small,—that it was the one black crow which, in the mephitic imagination of men like Morris, had grown to three.

Such are the facts anent the great journalistic Waterloo, or Perterloo—a harmless fisticuff such as happens in Texas a hundred times a day without being considered a news item by any legitimate journal. Instead of being "driven out of San Antonio in disgrace," as has been proclaimed by Ananias newspapers and whining preachers, I was on the streets of that city every day for three months after the difficulty. During that time the elite of San Antonio filled the opera house to hear me lecture, and the *Express* twice urged me to accept editorial employment on more favorable terms than formerly. All this must be as well known to the Revs. Slattery and Morris as to the citizens of San Antonio. This brace of ministerial blackguards exploit stale calumnies simply because they lack brains that can breed falsehoods to which they may play the father. Had God not ordained that they should be fools they would be very dangerous knaves.

But were I as cowardly as a fat-headed preacher who makes calumny and leg-pulling a profession, and guilty of every count in the great calendar of crime; had I been chased out of San Antonio by a cripple armed with a corn-stalk, and dismissed in disgrace by a dozen reputable dailies; were every charge preferred against me by men who are safe in their utter insignificance founded on fact, and every exaggeration thereof by sanctified thieves of reputation as true as the Synoptical Gospels, would that justify Joe Slattery in defaming women who are at least as good as his wife, or Dr. Burleson in driving out into the world the pregnant "ward of the Baptist church" and denouncing her as a chronic bawd? Is it any answer to the philippics of Demosthenes to point out that he threw away his shield and fled the foe? any answer to Tom Paine's terrible arraignment of the Christian cult to say that he died a miserable drunkard? any answer to the "Apostle's" plea for a stranger child to urge that he is no angel with peacock plumes for pinions? Truth is truth tho' told by the devil. The character of the "Apostle" is not the bone of contention. He hasn't been raped. Let us stick to the text—to poor little Antonia Teixeira and her Baptist bastard.

REVOLVERS, ROPES AND RELIGION

After being mobbed by a Baylor group, Brann returns to the affray with this smoking broadside. Within five months he was dead, by a bullet in the back.

I have just been enjoying the first holiday I have had in fifteen years. Owing to circumstances entirely beyond my control, I devoted the major part of the past month to digesting a couple of installments of Saving Grace presented by my Baptist brethren, and carefully rubbed in with revolvers and ropes, loaded canes and miscellaneous cudgels—with almost any old thing calculated to make a sinner reflect upon the status of his soul. That explains the shortcomings of the present issue of the Iconoclast. One cannot write philosophic essays while dallying with the Baptist faith. It were too much like mixing Websterian dignity with a cataleptoid convulsion, or sitting on a red ant hill and trying to look unconcerned. Here in Waco our religious zeal registers 600 in the shade, and when we hold a love-feast you can hear the unctuous echoes of our hosannahs from Tadmor in the Wilderness to the Pillars of Hercules. We believe with St. Paul that faith without works is dead; hence we gird up our loins with the sweet cestus of love, grab our guns and go awhooping forth to "capture the world for Christ." When we find a contumacious sinner we waste no time in theological controversy or moral suasion, but promptly round him up with a rope and bump his head, and we bump it hard. Why consume our energies "agonizing" with an emissary of Satan, explaining his error and striving by honied phrases to lead him into the light, when it is so much easier to seize him by pompadour and pantalettes and drag him bodily from the abyss? Some may complain that our Christian charity carries a razor edge, that we skim the cream off our milk of human kindness then put the can under an alkali pump before serving it to our customers as a prime article; but bless God! they can scarce expect to

"* * * be carried to the skies
On flowery beds of ease,
Whilst others fight to win the prize
And sail thro' bloody seas."

My Baptist brethren desired to send me as a missionary to foreign lands, and their invitation was so urgent, their expressions of regard so fervent that I am now wearing my head in a sling and trying to write with my left hand. Altho' they declared that I had an imperative "call" to go, and would tempt Providence by loitering longer than one short day, I concluded to remain in Waco and preach them a few more of my popular sermons from that favorite text, "If ye forgive not men their trespasses, neither will your Father forgive your trespasses." It is quite possible that a few heathen will go to hell whom I might enable to find the river route to heaven, but I believe in doing the duty that lies next my hand—in first saving the heathen right here at home.

But enough of persiflage; now for cold facts. In all candor, I would cheerful ignore the recent disgraceful occurrences in this city could I do so in justice to the South in general and to Texas in particular. I have no revenge to gratify, no more feeling in the matter than tho' the assault had been made upon an utter stranger. It is quite true that for a time I was eager to call my assailants out one by one and settle the affair after the manner of our fathers; but being credibly informed that instead of honoring a cartel, they would make it the basis of a legal complaint and send me to the penitentiary, and having no desire to enact the role of the street assassin, I became once more a law-abiding citizen. Truth to tell, there's not one of the whole cowardly tribe who's worth a charge of buckshot, who deserves so much honor as being sent to hell by a white man's hand. If Socrates was poisoned and Christ was crucified for telling unpalatable truths to the splenetic-hearted hypocrites of their time, it would ill become me to complain of a milder martyrdom for a like offense. It may be urged that having been accused of the heinous crime of slandering young ladies, and twice beset on that pretext by armed thugs, I owe it to myself to make some explanation satisfactory to the public. Not at all; from my youth up noble womanhood has been the very god of my idolatry; and now that I have reached the noon of life, if the reputation which I have honestly earned as a faithful defender of the vestal fires, can be blown adown the wind by the rank breath of lying rascals, I would not put forth a hand to check its flight. If old scars received while defending woman's name and fame in paths of peril which my traducers dare not tread, fail to speak for me, then to hell with the world, and let its harlot tongue wag howsoever it will. Never but once did I stoop to refute a cowardly falsehood circulated about myself. I was younger then—had not learned that public opinion is a notorious bawd, that "nailing a lie" but accentuates its circulation. Unfortunately, the recent assaults upon me are not altogether my private concern. They were armed protests against a fundamental principle of this Republic—freedom of the press. They are being cited by ill advised or malicious persons as evidence of "Southern Savagery.' They are calculated, if suffered to go unexplained, to cast reproach upon revealed religion. They were futile but brutal attempts in the last decade of the Nineteenth century to suppress truth by terror, to conceal the iniquities of a sectarian college by beating to death the only journalist who dared to raise his voice in protest. They were appeals to Judge Lynch to strangle exposure, hence it is imperative that the blame be placed where it properly belongs; not upon the South, which unqualifiedly condemns it; not upon the Baptist church, which indignantly repudiates it; but upon a little coterie of white-livered, black-hearted hypocrites, any of whom could look thro' a keyhole with both eyes at once, a majority of whom are avowed sympathizers with or active members of that unamerican organization known to infamy as the A. P. A. The same old God-forsaken gang of moral perverts and intellectual misfits who more than two years ago brought a Canadian courtesan and an unfrocked priest to Waco to lecture on A. P. Aism, and who threatened at one of these buzzard-feasts to rob me for calling the latter a cowardly liar, were responsible for my being dragged with a rope by several hundred hoodlums up and down a Baptist college campus in this city Oct. 2, and for the brutal assault upon me five days later by a pack of would-be assassins who waited until my back was unsuspectingly turned before they had the nerve to get out their guns. I can overlook the assault made by the college students, altho' most of them were grown men, because they were encouraged thereto by their elders. I have positively refused to prosecute them; but the last assault was led by a shyster lawyer of middle-age, a so-called "judge," a member of the board of managers of Baylor. I am seeking no trouble with any of them—they are perfectly safe in so far as I am concerned; still if the latter gang are not satisfied with their cowardly crime, if they regret that they were beaten off ere they quite succeeded in sending me to Kingdom Come, they have only to notify me where and when they can be found alone, and I'll give the whole accursed mob a show for its money. I'm too slight for a slugger—cannot lick a herd of steers with one pair o' hands; but I can make a shotgun sing Come to Christ. I am credibly informed that "at least half a dozen" of my meek and lowly Baptist brethren are but awaiting an opportunity to assassinate me, and that if successful they will plead in extenuation that I "have slandered Southern women." I walk the streets of Waco day by day, and I walk them alone. Let these cur-ristians shoot me in the back if they dare, then plead that damning lie as excuse for their craven cowardice. If the decent people of this community fail to chase them to their holes and feed their viscera to the dogs, then I'd rather be dead and in hades forever than alive in Waco a single day.

The claim set up by my assailants that I had slandered the female students of Baylor University is a malicious calumny, was but made a lying pretext for the attacks. That my article in the October Iconoclast did *not* impeach the character of the Baylor girls is amply evidenced by the fact that my offer to leave the matter to the decision of a committee of reputable business men, to abjectly apologize and donate $500 to any charity these gentlemen might name in case their decision was against me, was flatly refused. "The honor of young ladies is not a proper subject for arbitration," I was told. Quite true; but the proper construction of an article which is made a pretext for mob violence, *is* a proper matter for cool-headed and disinterested parties to pass upon. The Baylorians insisted upon being judge, jury and executioner—proof positive that they well knew the article would not stand the arbitrary construction they had placed upon it. After the first outbreak the Baylor bullies of the lost manhood stripe and their milk-sick apologists held a windy powwow in a Baptist church, and there bipedal brutes with beards, creatures who have thus far succeeded in dodging the insane asylum, whom an inscrutable Providence has kept out of the penitentiary to ornament the amen-corner—many of whom do not pretend to pay their bills, some of whom owe me for the very meat upon the bones of their scorbutic brats—branded me as a falsifier while solemnly protesting that they had never read a line of my paper. They proclaimed in stentor tones and pigeon-English that would have broken the heart of Lindley Murray, that I was a defamer of womanhood—while confessing that they didn't know whether I had ever mentioned a female. They howled that they "were willing to sign Brann's death-warrant"—on mere hearsay. These intellectual eunuchs, who couldn't father an idea if cast bodily into the womb of the goddess of wisdom, declared positively that I would be permitted to print nothing more about their berluved Baylor—and that without knowing whether I had advertised it over two continents as an oasis in a moral Sahara or a snakehole in the Dismal Swamp. It was a beautiful, a refreshing sight, this practical approval of mob violence by unfledged ministers on the campus of a Baptist college, this raucous tommyrot about death-warrants and ropes, this sawing of the air and chewing of the rag by people so d—d ignorant that they couldn't find either end of themselves in the dark, this chortling over the fact that one desk-emaciated welter-weight had been caught unawares and trampled upon by a sanctified mob—a refreshing sight I say, in a temple consecrated to that Christ who forgave even his enemies from the cross! But every man at that meeting who said he never read the Iconoclast deliberately lied. The Baptists all read it. Some subscribe and pay for it like gentlemen, some buy it, some borrow it, and the rest steal it from the newsstands. The greatest trouble I have is to prevent Baptist preachers spoiling my local sale by telling everybody in town what the Iconoclast contains before the revised proof-sheets are read. It is but fair to say, however, that the Baptists were not alone to blame. Much of the noise was made by a lot of tickey-tailed little politicians who have no more religion than a rabbit, but who were trying to open a popular jack-pot with a jimmy. Some of the brawlers were self-seeking business men of the Sanger-Rotan type, willing to coin blood into boodle, ready to slander Deity for a plugged dime, anxious to avert a Baptist boycott by emitting a deal of stinking breath. These two big financial ducks in a provincial mud-puddle have had entirely too much to say. When the present lecture season is over; when I get the Baptist mob thoroughly cowed; when I can walk the streets without expecting every moment to get shot from a stairway or double-banked by the meek and lowly followers of the Messiah; when I have time to amuse myself with trifles, I'll sue this brace of Smart Alecs for $20,000 each for deliberate defamation of character, and if I recover the money I'll use it to make a partial payment on the grocery bills of the rest of the gang. Intellectual pigmies who accumulate much cash by trading in tape or tripe in a country town are quite apt to become too big for their britches and require to be taken down a peg or two, to be taught their place. They sometimes have the nickel-plated nerve to play Rhadamanthus to the purveyors of brains—swell up like unclean toads and conceive themselves to be in "select society." Why Sanger and Rotan actually imagine themselves of more importance in this community than Judge Gerald and Waller Baker; yet you could scrape enough intellect from under Gerald's toenails to build 'em both, while Baker forgets more every fifteen minutes than they have learned since they were born. The meeting held at the Baptist church to ratify the outrage was composed of a lot of self-seekers and whining hypocrites, half of whom would sell their souls for a copper cent and throw in their risen Lord as lagniappe. It was a mob that writhed and wriggled in its own putridity like so many maggots, while the local press cowered before its impotent wrath like young skye-terriers before a skunk. If I couldn't beget better men with the help of a Digger Indian harem I'd take to the woods and never again look upon the face of woman. It was a glorious sight to see these "pore mizzuble wurrums of the dust" spraining their yarn galluses trying to hurl the writhen bolts of Olympian Jove—and now, bellyaching because hit in the umbilicus with their own boomerang. The second assault, more brutal and cowardly than the first, followed as the logical sequence of that powwow of pietists, peddlers and politicians. The utterances of that congregation of unclean adders, the resolutions adopted by that sanctified body of deadbeats in the sanctum sanctorum of the Baptists, was a bid for blood—injected the idea into the warty heads of a trio of thugs that by waylaying and beating me to death they would pass into history as heroes.

Then the real manhood of Waco rose *en masse* and laid down the law in no uncertain language to the hungry hypocrites and their Baylorian hoodlums. They declared that religious intolerance would no longer be permitted to terrorize this town. Fearing just retribution at the hands of the citizens, Baylor called out its three military companies and mounted guard with rifles furnished by the government, while the very girls in whose name they had dragged me around the college campus with a rope, laughed them to scorn and sent me flowers—and the password of the bold sojer boys. One young lady writes: "The password for the night is 'Napoleon.' Our bold soldiers halted a milk wagon at daylight this morning. Probably they thought Brann was concealed in one of the cans with his bowie-knife." Half a dozen men armed with cannon-crackers could have chased the brave mellish into the Brazos and danced with the Baylor girls till daybreak—and I suspect that the latter would have enjoyed the lark. For a third of a century the bigotry of a lot of water moccasins had been the supreme law of this land. To obtain an office the politician had to crawl to it on his marrow-bones and slavishly obey its behests. To obtain trade the merchant had to sneeze whenever it took snuff. To obtain patronage the local publisher had to make it the absolute dictator of his policy. Like Jehushran, it "waxed fat and kicked"—until it got its legs tied in a double bow-knot around its own neck. Its tyranny became insupportable, murderous, there was a new declaration of American independence, and now this J. Caesar that erstwhile did bestride Central Texas like a colossus, is more humble than Uriah Heep. And what were the A. P. Apes of Waco doing while honest men were raising the standard of revolt and chasing the Baptist hierarchy into its hole? Were they in the front rank shouting their war-cry of "no union of church and state"—the "little red school-house" rampant on their orange-colored rag? Not exactly. They had sneaked off to some bat cave to plot against the whites, to protest against the proceedings of their fellow citizens. Had a Baptist editor been mobbed on the campus of a Catholic college they would have howled a lung out about Popish tyranny, stood on their heads and fanned themselves with their own shirt-tails.

The faculty of Baylor protest that they did all in their power to prevent the brutal outbreak. They confess, however, that it had been brewing all day, yet they neglected to notify either myself or the sheriff. Before me is a Lake Charles, La., paper, in which a letter from one of the scabs who participated in the first attack, is published. He says: *"The faculty did not say do it, or not do it."* And that's about the size of it. That the students were encouraged by one or more members of the board of trustees can be demonstrated beyond the peradventure of a doubt. All the stale bath water in all the Baptist tanks this side Perdition cannot wash the conviction from the public mind that the Baylor management was behind that howling mob. The second assault was *led* by a trustee, a member of the board of managers; and this after I had stated positively in the local press that I meant no disparagement of the young ladies—that it was the administration of the University I was after. In the October Iconoclast I expressed the fervent hope that no more young ladies would be debauched at Baylor. That constituted the ostensible *casus belli.* Do the trustees of Baylor dare deny that such things *have* occurred at that "storm center of misinformation" and ministerial manufactory? If so, they are a precious long time putting me to the proof in the courts of this country. Texas has an iron-clad criminal libel law, and I suspect that I could pay a judgment for damages in any reasonable sum without spraining my credit or bankrupting the Iconoclast. If they have not the chilled-steel hardihood to deny that girls have been debauched at Baylor—if by their resounding silence anent this matter they mean to give assent—what then? Do they hope that more girls *will* be ruined there? Are they angry because I would preserve maidenly purity? They may take either horn of the dilemma they like; but I beg to state that the issue here raised cannot be obscured by dragging me around with a rope. When Jonah was caught in a scheme of vindictive rascality he thought he "did well to be angry." The best thing the Baylorites can do is to 'fess up and reform—it's too late in the century to suppress truth with six-shooters. I have heard of no "deplorable accidents" at Add-Ran, the Christian college, consequently it has no complaints to file against the Iconoclast. The Convent of the Sacred Heart gets along somehow without "mishaps," and even Paul Quinn, the colored college, is graduating no "missionaries" for Hungry Hill. Because some girls go wrong at an institution for the promotion of ignorance, it by no means follows that all, or any considerable number thereof are deficient in morality. I doubt not that a vast majority of the female students at Baylor, past and present, are pure as the flowers that bloom above the green glacier; but some have fallen, and the conclusion is inevitable that they were not properly protected from the wiles of the world. I care not how noble-minded, how pure of heart a girl may be, if she is committed when young and inexperienced to a college where both sexes are received, it becomes the imperativ duty of the management to render one false step impossible. When the president of a pretentious sectarian institute must plead with the public that he had "wept and prayed over" a 14-year-old girl, but was powerless to prevent her rushing headlong to ruin; when at a grand rally of the faithful to condemn a well-meant criticism and encourage mob violence, an old he-goat who couldn't get trusted at the corner grocery for a pound of soap, confesses to more than the Iconoclast had charged, by saying that some *accidents* had occurred at the college, it were well for mothers to look carefully to its management and note its discipline before entrusting it with their young daughters. "Accidents," indeed! Criminal negligence would be a more appropriate name. A university consecrated to the Baptist Christ, whose trustees lead cowardly assaults upon law-abiding citizens and beat them with bludgeons after they are insensible; whose faculty know that mob violence is contemplated yet fail to report it to the police; whose students enter the home of a man for the purpose of dragging him by force and with drawn pistols from the presence of his family (the Baylor thugs had the impudence to invade my home in search of me before finding me in the city)—such an institution, I say, is not a proper guardian for any youth whose father doesn't desire to see him land in the Baptist pulpit or the penitentiary. I have been publicly warned on pain of death, and heaven alone knows what hereafter, not to speak "disrespectfully" of Baylor; but I feel in duty bound to caution parents against committing their children to such a pestiferous plague-spot, such a running sore upon the body social.

Not only has Baylor demonstrated its unworthiness to be the custodian of young people of either sex, but such unworthiness has been proclaimed in the public prints by Dr. Rufus C. Burleson, who served as its president for almost half a century. I insisted that the salaries paid the faculty at Baylor were insufficient to command the services of first-class educators, and that those entrusted with the duty of selecting teachers were incapable of correctly estimating the educational qualifications of others. Dr. Burleson goes far beyond that, expressly declaring in the Dallas *News* that a majority of the present board of managers are not college educated, that for them to properly administer discipline and make wise selection of teachers is "simply impossible." What, in God's name, can be expected of an institution containing several hundred young people of both sexes, if it be deficient in discipline? Of what earthly use is a University if it be not provided with a wisely selected faculty? It now remains to be seen whether the Baptist brethren will mob Dr. Burleson—or sneak up behind him with an assortment of clubs and six-shooters! But that is not the worst that Dr. Burleson says. In a published letter of his now before me he denounces Dr. B. H. Carroll, chairman of the board of trustees and present high muck-a-muck of Baylor, as an ingrate, a self-seeker, a mischief-maker and an irremediable liar! Now if Burleson is telling the truth—and I am not prepared to dispute his statements—what can we expect of a University managed by such a man? I am frank to confess that I did not suspect Bro. Carroll to be quite so bad. I knew that he was an intellectual dugout spreading the canvas of a seventy-four, that there was precious little to him but gab and gall; but I did not suppose that he was an habitual falsifier and guilty of base ingratitude. I really hope that Dr. Burleson may be mistaken—that the new boss of Baylor has not contracted such a habit of lying that it is utterly impossible for him to tell the truth. I should dislike to believe all that is said about each other by the two factions of my Baptist brethren now struggling for the control of Baylor. According to Carroll, Dr. Burleson, president emeritus, ought to be in the penitentiary; according to Burleson, Carroll is not a fit associate for a brindle cow. "Speak disrespectfully of Baylor and die!" Good Lord! were I to repeat one-half that the Baylor factions are saying about each other I'd wreck the state. Time was when the faculty of Baylor was the pride of the South. Those were the days when many of the noblest men and women of Texas were educated within its walls. They love their *alma mater,* not for what she is, but for what she was. The old professors are gone, have been supplanted in great part by a lot of priorient little preachers, selected by a board of trustees, half of whom couldn't tell a Greek root from a rutabaga, *pons asinorum* from Balaam's ass. Dr. Burleson seems to be of the opinion that a majority of the Baylorian managers were educated in a mule-pen and dismissed without a diploma—couldn't tell whether a man were construing Catullus into Sanskrit or pronouncing in Piute a panegyric on a baked pup. Were I not *persona non grata* I would like to witness the classroom performances of these young professors—chosen with owlish gravity by men who cannot write *deer sur* without the expenditure of enough nervo-muscular energy to raise a cotton crop, chewing off the tips of their tongues and blotting the paper with their proboscides. Yet for offering to open a night school for the benefit of the Baylorian faculty I was mobbed; for intimating that the board of managers had not socked with old Socrates and ripped with old Euripides I was assaulted by one of their number and his brave body guard and beaten with six-shooters and bludgeons until I was insensible.

It is not my present purpose to drag forth all the grisly skeletons of Baylor and make them dance for the amusement of the multitude. I have yielded to the urgent appeals of my friends to let the institution down easy, to cast a little kerosene on the troubled waters, to hold out the olive branch to Baylor. Besides, I already have more holes in my head than nature intended, and am not particularly anxious to increase the assortment. Let what is hidden from public ken so remain until that great incubator of Christian charity, that ganglion of brotherly love attempts to redeem its long-standing promise to land me in the penitentiary for criminal libel. It could serve no good purpose at present to trace out here the history of those "accidents" so feelingly referred to at the ratification of the Brann roundup—would but cause cheeks to flame and hearts to break. I would not destroy Baylor; I would make it better. I would deprive the ignorant and vicious of control. I would expel all the hoodlums whose brutality and cowardice have disgraced it. I would place at its head a thorough educator and strict disciplinarian, a man of broad views and who sets a good example by paying his bills. I would make its diplomas badges of honor as in the old days, instead of certificates of illiteracy at which public school children laugh. No, I do not want the presidency—there are enough perspiring Christians for revenue only quarreling and lying about each other because of that beggarly plum already. For months past it has given every Baptist journal in the state a hot-box, has filled every little preacher's head with all the petty intrigues of peanut politics. If one-half that the leaders of the factions, now warring over this pitiful $5 per diem bone, say about each other be true—and I have no evidence to the contrary—they would disgrace a boozing ken on Boiler avenue. I do not mean to say that all Texas Baptists are bad:

at least 50 per cent of them are broad-gauge, tolerant, intelligent; the remainder are small-bore bigots upon whom nature put heads, as Dean Swift would say, "Solely for the sake of conformity."

Baylor and the Baptists complain that the Iconoclast has "persecuted them until it has become unbearable." Bless God! who began this thing? Before the Iconoclast was three days old it was boycotted by the hydrocephalous sect. As it grew fat on that kind of fodder, ex-Priest Slattery and his ex-*none* wife were brought hither to lecture on A. P. Aism, and incidentally make the town too caloric for my comfort. The Baptists took their wives and daughters to listen to Slattery's foul lies about the convents and the confessional, the Pope and "his Waco Apostle," and his most infamous utterances were applauded to the echo. They sent their wives and daughters to hear the Slattery female defame women who had given up the pleasures of the world and were devoting their lives to the reclamation of such unclean creatures as herself. Slattery's last harangue was delivered to men only and the house was packed with Baptists and Baylorites at half-a-dollar a head. The so-called lecture was the foulest thing that ever fell from the lips of mortal man, yet his audience gloated over it and rolled his putrid falsehoods as sweet morsels under its tongue. Unable to restrain my indignation, I arose and denounced his every utterance as a malicious lie. Immediately the audience yelled, "Throw him out! Down with him! Smash him!" I chanced to have my back near the side-wall, and that's why I wasn't mobbed—the cowardly crew couldn't get *behind* me. They suspected that I'd make an angel of the first sanctified galloot who attempted to place his paws upon me, and none cared to draw on his celestial bank account. That's the identical gang which has the immaculate gall to accuse me of defaming virtuous women—the same gang which applauded Slattery for calling convents priestly harems wants me killed for expressing the hope that no more young girls will be debauched at Baylor.

Scarce had Baylor's applause of Slattery and his woman died away; scarce had it ceased to gloat over the "iniquities" of convent schools and priestly harems; scarce had it ceased chuckling over the crimes of "the Scarlet Woman," ere the police discovered that the duly ordained "ward of the Baptist church," who was being educated at Baylor University for missionary work among the heathen Catholics of Brazil, was in a dreadfully "delicate condition." She was brought from Brazil at the tender age of 11 years by a returning missionary, she was formally adopted by the Baptist church, she was consecrated to the salvation of souls and placed at Baylor to be educated. She was under the special supervision of the president and was a member of his own household—yet at 14 years of age she became enceinte! Did Baylor pity and protect her? Did it strive to secure the punishment of the seducer? Not exactly. It fired her out and made no complaint to the police. When the latter discovered her and she was required by the court to account for her condition she stated that she had been forcibly despoiled by a young man about town on the premises of Baylor's president. It chanced that this young man was brother to the president's son-in-law, and the whole influence of Baylor was brought to bear to clear the accused! The son-in-law, who is a Baptist preacher and editor (as well as other things not necessary to mention) strove to make her confess that her guilty paramour was a pickaninny—wanted the world to believe that orphan girls committed to the care of that great Baptist college might become enceinte by coons! Yet the Baylor students didn't mob him—none of its trustees laid in wait for him and slammed him over the head with a six-shooter. The girl soon put a white babe in evidence—a pretty little two-pound Baylorian diploma! The doctors declared that she had been raped, and the case looked ugly for the accused. The child died. The ignorant little mother wanted money to go to Memphis—and first thing we knew she had signed a "retraction" and had a ticket to Mike Connolly's town. Who bought it—and why? Damfino. The defendant was acquitted of the charge of rape—the age of consent in Texas being 12 years at that time; but whether she was raped or seduced, the infamy occurred at Baylor University. That's *one* of the "deplorable accidents;" but it is not the only one you will please not forget to remember. Reads like a fairy story, doesn't it? But the law doesn't permit Texas editors to tell fairy tales of that type. No doubt the man who has the audacity to breathe a hope that no more girls will be debauched at Baylor deserves to die. Dr. Burleson, in the fulness of his Baptist charity, branded the unfortunate girl as a natural bawd. I don't know about that; but I do know that after she got beyond Baylorian influences she married and began leading a respectable life.

Defamer of womanhood? Get the sawlogs out of your own eyes, brethren, before howling over the micrococci in the optics of others. For three years past Baptist preachers all over this land of Christ have been telling their congregations that the Iconoclast is read only by depraved people,—chiefly criminals and courtesans—and that despite the fact that the names of thousands of the noblest men and women of America are on its subscription books. During the past three years the Iconoclast has had upon its books the names of more than a thousand ministers, representing every denomination. Are these men criminals and their wives courtesans? Has any little Baptist parson been rounded up with a rope for proclaiming them as such from the pulpit? When a deserted babe was found in the street and carried by the Sisters to the convent, was Jehovah Boanerges Cranfill,—organ grinder for the Baylor bosses—mobbed by the Catholics for saying that it probably came *out* of the convent? Now, you people keep down the narrative of your nether garment and apply a hot mush poultice to your impudence. The Iconoclast is only tickling you with snipe-shot now; but don't forget for one moment that it has buck a plenty in its belt.

A word to the lady students of Baylor: Young ladies, this controversy does not in the least concern you. The Iconoclast has never questioned your good character. You are young, however, and mischievous people have led some of you to believe that it has done so. If you so believe, I am as much in duty bound to apologize as tho' I had really and intentionally wronged you. A gentleman should ever hasten to apologize to ladies who feel aggrieved; hence I sincerely crave your pardon for having printed the article which gave you offense. Upon learning that you read into it a meaning which I did not intend, I stopped the presses and curtailed the circulation of the October number as much as possible, proving my sincerity by pecuniary sacrifice. I would not for the wealth of this world either do you a willful injustice, or have you believe me capable of such a crime. May you prosper in your studies, graduate with honor and bestow your hands upon men worthy of noble women.

* * *

P. S. In looking over the foregoing since it was put in type, I suspect that I have been a trifle too hard on some of those who met to ratify the action of the first mob and publicly brand me as a defamer of women. I would not do my deadliest enemy an injustice—two wrongs do not make a right; hence I concede that perhaps half of those present pay their debts and make a reasonable effort to be decent. If God neglected to bless them with brains, that is their misfortune instead of their fault. Let it go at that. They have had their say, I've had mine, and right here I drop the subject until another attempt is made to run me out of town. I make this concession, not that Baylor deserves it, but at the earnest request of the law-abiding element of this city.

SPEAKING OF GALL

Here is one of Brann's most popular platform speeches, delivered to audiences all across the South. It is highly representative of Iconoclast style.

Gall is a bitter subject, and I shall waste no time selecting sweet words in which to handle it. There's no surplus of sweet words in my vocabulary anyhow. I have never yet been able to rent my mouth for a taffy mill. Webster gives several definitions of Gall; but the good old etymologist was gathered to his fathers long before the word attained its full development and assumed an honored place in the slang vernacular of the day. It was needed. It fills what editors sometimes call "a long-felt want." Gall is sublimated audacity, transcendent impudence, immaculate nerve, triple-plated cheek, brass in solid slugs. It is what enables a man to borrow five dollars of you, forget to repay it, then touch you for twenty more. It is what makes it possible for a woman to borrow her neighbor's best bonnet, then complain because it isn't the latest style or doesn't suit her particular type of beauty. It is what causes people to pour their troubles into the ears of passing acquaintances instead of reserving them for home consumption. It is what makes a man aspire to the governorship, or to air his asininity in the Congress of the United States when he should be fiddling on a stick of cordwood with an able-bodied buck-saw. It is what leads a feather-headed fop, with no fortune but his folly, no prospects but poverty—who lacks business ability to find bread for himself—to mention marriage to a young lady reared in luxury, to ask her to leave the house of her father and help him fill the land with fools. Gall is what spoils so many good ditchers and delvers to make peanut politicians and putty-headed professional men. It is what puts so many men in the pulpit who could serve their Saviour much better planting the mild-eyed potato or harvesting the useful hoop-pole. It is what causes so many young ladies to rush into literature instead of the laundry—to become poets of passion instead of authors of pie.

Gall is a very common ailment. In fact, a man without a liberal supply of it is likely to be as lonesome in this land as a consistent Christian at a modern camp-meeting, or a gold-bug Democrat in Texas. Nearly everybody has it and is actually proud of it. When a young man is first afflicted with the tender passion; when he is in the throes of the mysterious mental aberration that would cause him to climb a mesquite bush and lasso the moon for his inamorata if she chanced to admire it, he is apt to think it love that makes the world go round. Later he learns that Gall is the social dynamics—the force that causes humanity to arise and hump itself.

Gall has got the world grabbed. Politics is now a high-class play, whose pawns are power and plunder; business is becoming but a gouge-game wherein success hallows any means. Our mighty men are our most successful marauders; our social favorites minister in the temple of Mammon, our pillar of cloud by day and of fire by night the follies and foibles of the "Four Hundred," our God the Golden Calf. The standard by which society now measures men is the purse; that by which it gauges greatness the volume of foolish sound which the aspirant for immortal honors succeeds in setting afloat, little caring whether it be such celestial harp music as caused Thebe's walls to rise, or the discordant bray of the ram's horn which made Jericho's to fall. This century, which proudly boasts itself "heir to all the ages and foremost in the files of time," doffs its beaver to brazen effrontery, burns its sweetest incense on the unhallowed shrine of pompous humbuggery, while modest merit is in a more pitiable predicament than the traditional tomcat in Tartarus without teeth or toenails.

We make manifest our immeasurable Gall by proclaiming from the housetops that, of all the ages which have passed o'er the hoary head of Mother Earth, the present stands pre-eminent; that of all the numberless cycles of Time's mighty pageant there was none like unto it—no, not one. And I sincerely hope there wasn't. Perhaps that which induced the Deity to repent him that he had made man and send a deluge to soak some of the devilment out of him, was the nearest approach to it. We imagine that because we have the electric telegraph and the nickel-plated dude, the printing press and the campaign lie, the locomotive and the scandal in high life; that because we now roast our political opponent instead of the guileless young missionary, and rob our friends by secret fraud instead of despoiling our foes by open force, that we are the people *par-excellence* and the Lord must be proud of us.

Progress and improvement are not always synonyms. A people may grow in Gall instead of grace. I measure a century by its men rather than by its machines, and we have not, since civilization took its boasted leap forward, produced a Socrates or a Shakespeare, a Phidias or an Angelo, a Confucius or a Christ. This century runs chiefly to Talmages and Deacon Twogoods, pauper dukes and divorce courts—intellectual soup and silk lingerie.

* * *

The poets no longer sing of the immortal gods, of war and sacrifice, while the flame mounts to manhood's cheek, red as the fires of Troy: They twitter of lovies and dovies, of posies and goose-liver pie, while pretty men applaud and sentimental maids get moonsick. Cincinnatus no longer waits for the office to seek the man: He sells his brace of bullocks and buys a political boom. No more the Spartan mother gives her long black hair for bowstrings: She blondines it, paints, powders and tries to pass as the younger sister of her eldest daughter. The Norse viking no longer plows the unknown wave, his heart wilder than the wat'ry waste, his arm stronger than tempered steel: He comes to America and starts a saloon. No more the untamed Irish king caroms on the Saxon invader with a seasoned shillalah: He gets on the police force and helps "run the machine," or clubs the head off the harmless married man who won't go home till morning. In these degenerate days the philosopher retires not to the desert, and there, by meditation most profound, wrings from the secret treasure-house of his own superior soul, jewels to adorn his age and enrich the world: He mixes an impossible plot with a little pessimism, adds a dude and a woman whose moral character has seen better days, spills the nauseous compound on the public as a "philosophical novel" and works the press for puffs. Indeed we're progressing; going onward and upward—like the belled buzzard dodging a divorce scandal. Greece had her Pericles, but it was left for us to produce a Parkhurst. Rome had her Cicero and her Caesar, but was never equal to a Culberson or a Corbett. The princes of old conquered the earth, but the modern plutocrats put a mortgage on it. Cleopatra drank pearls dissolved in wine, but whisky straight is said to be good enough for some of her successors. Samson slew the Philistines with a jawbone of an ass; but a modern politician, employing the self-same weapon, would have got 'em to elect him governor. We've got no Helen of Troy; but our "Hell'n Blazes" is a bird o' the same feather. We've got to yield the palm in poetry and philosophy, art and architecture; but when it comes to building political platforms that straddle every important issue and slinging princely style on a pauper income we're out of sight.

How can the acorn become a mighty forest monarch if planted in a pint pot and crossed with a fuzzy-wuzzy chrysanthemum? How can the Numidian lion's whelp become a king of beasts if reared in a cage and fed on cold potatoes, muzzled and made to dance to popular music? How can the superior soul expand until it becomes all-embracing, god-like, a universe in itself, in which rings sweet sphere-music and rolls Jovinian thunder—in which blazes true Promethean fire instead of smoulders the sulphurous caloric of the nether world—when its metes and bounds are irrevocably fixed for it—when it can only grow in certain prescribed directions, painfully mapped out for it by bumptious pismires who imagine that their little heads constitute the intellectual Cosmos?

* * *

Hamlet, Prince of Denmark, lamented that he lacked Gall; but the melancholy Dane was dead years before the present generation of titled snobs appeared upon the scene. None of the princes or dukes of the present day appear to be short on Gall; none of the nobility seem to be suffering for lack of it. Not long ago a little Duke who owes his title to the fact that his great-grand-aunt was the paramour of a half-wit prince, kindly condescended to marry an American girl to recoup his failing fortunes. A little French guy whose brains are worth about two cents a pound—for soap-grease—put up a Confederate-bond title for the highest bidder and was bought in like a hairless Mexican pup by an American plutocrat. Now half-a-dozen more little pauper princelings and decadent dukelings are trying to trade their worthless coronets for American cash. But the fact that many a man boasting of his American sovereignty will dicker with a titled young duke, instead of using the forecastle of a No. 9 foot to drive his spinal column up thro' his plug-hat like a presidential lightning-rod; will actually purchase for his daughter some disgusting little title upon which rests the fateful bar-sinister of a woman's shame, and is encumbered by a dizzy young dude, too lazy to work and too cowardly to steal —too everlastingly "ornery" to raise a respectful crop of wild oats—proves that the young lollipop lordlings haven't a monopoly of the Gall of the Globe.

* * *

A most shameful exhibition of Gall is the practice now coming into vogue with certain society ladies of encouraging newspapers to puff their charms—even paying them so much a line for fulsome praise. Not a few metropolitan papers reap a handsome profit by puffing society buds whom their fond parents are eager to place on the matrimonial market, hoping that they will "make good matches;" in other words, that they will marry money—its possessors being thrown in as *pelon.* Even married women, who are long on shekels but short on sense, sometimes pay big prices to get their portraits in the public prints—accompanied by puffs that would give a buzzard a bilious attack.

But the gall of the girl who puts her picture in the papers, accompanied by a paid puff of her "purty," scarce equals that of the conceited maid who imagines she has only to look at a man and giggle a few times to "mash him cold"—to get his palpitating heart on a buckskin string and swing it hither-and-yon at pleasure. How the great he-world does suffer at the hands of those heartless young coquettes—if half it tells 'em be true! David said in his haste that all men are liars. And had he carefully considered the matter he would have come to the same conclusion. Washington may have told his father the truth about that cherry tree; but later in life he became entirely too popular with the ladies for a man unable to lie.

It is natural for men to pay court to a pretty woman as for flies to buzz about a molasses barrel; but not every fly that buzzes expects to get stuck, I beg to state. The man who doesn't tell every woman who will listen to him—excepting, perhaps, his wife—that she's pretty as a peri, even tho' she be homely enough to frighten a mugwump out of a fat federal office; that she's got his heart grabbed; that he lives only in the studied sunshine of her store-teeth smile and is hungering for an opportunity to die for her dear sake—well, he's an angel, and he-seraphs are almighty scarce I beg of you to believe. Since Adonis died and Joseph was gathered to his fathers none have appeared that I am aware of. These young gentlemen were all right, I suppose; but I'd like to see either of them get elected now-a-days on the Democratic ticket in Texas.

But feminine conceit, fed on flattery, were as milk-shake unto mescal, as a kiss by mail to one by moonlight compared with the insufferable egotism of the "pretty man" who puts his moustache up in curl-papers and perfumes his pompadour; who primps and postures before an amorous looking-glass and imagines that all Eve's daughters are trying to abduct him. . Whenever I meet one of these male irresistibles I'm forcibly reminded that the Almighty made man out of mud—and not very good mud at that. The two-legged he-thing who makes a clothes-horse of himself and poses on the street corner perfumed like an emancipation day picnic; who ogles a pretty woman until the crimson creeps into her cheek, then prides himself on having captured her heart like the boy caught the itch,—because he couldn't help it—when she's only blushing for the mother who bore the pitiful parody of manhood; who imagines that every maid who deigns to waste a smile on him is sighing her soul out for his sweet sake, has allowed his Gall to go to his head and curdle his brains.

* * *

More than a moiety of our so-called great men are but featherless geese, possessing a superabundance of Gall—creatures of chance who ride like driftwood on the crest of a wave raised by forces they cannot comprehend; but they ride, and the world applauds them while it tramples better men beneath its brutal feet. Greatness and Gall, genius and goose-speech, sound and sense have become synonyms. If you fall on the wrong side of the market men will quote the proverb about a fool and his money; if on the right side you're a Napoleon of finance. Lead a successful revolt and you are a pure patriot whose memory should be preserved to latest posterity; head an unsuccessful uprising and you are a miserable rebel who should have been hanged. "Nothing succeeds like success." Had the Christian religion failed to take root, Judas Iscariot would have been commemorated in the archives of Rome as one who helped stamp out the hateful heresy, and had Washington got the worst of it in his go with Cornwallis he would have passed into history as a second Jack Cade.

Alexander of Macedon was great, as measured by the world's standard of eminence. After two-and-twenty centuries our very babes prattle of this bloody butcher, and even his horse has been enshrined in history. In our own day Father Damien left kindred and country and went forth to die for the miserable lepers in the mid-Pacific, but he is already forgotten—his name and fame have faded from the minds of men. Yet greater and grander than all the blood-stained princes and potentates of earth; nobler, more god-like than all the proud prelates that ever aired their turgid eloquence at Christian conference or ecumenical council was that young priest; but no cenotaph rises to commemorate his sacrifice—silent as his own sealed lips is the trumpet of fame.

But for Gall of the A1, triple-X brand, commend me to the little pot-house politician who poses as a political prophet and points out to wiser men their public duties. We have today in this land of the free and home of the crank, thousands of self-important little personages who know as little of political economy as a parrot of the power of prayer, prating learnedly of free-trade or protection, greenbackism or metallic money. Men who couldn't tell a fundamental principle from their funny-bone, an economic thesis from a hot tamale—who don't know whether Ricardo was an economist or a corn-doctor—evolve from their empty ignorance new systems of "saving the country," and defend them with the dogmatic assurance of a nigger preacher describing the devil—make gorgeous displays of their Gall. I have noticed that, as a rule, the less a man knows of the science of government the crazier he is to go to congress. About half the young statesmen who break into the legislature imagine that Roger Q. Mills wrote the Science of Economics, and that Jefferson Davis was the father of Democracy.

But the Gall is not confined to the little fellows—the big political M D's have their due proportion. The remedies they prescribe for Uncle Sam's ailments remind me of the panaceas put on the market by the patent-medicine men—warranted to cure everything, from a case of cholera-morbus to an epidemic of poor relations. We have one school of practitioners prescribing free-trade as a sure-cure for every industrial ill, another a more drastic system of protection. One assures us that the silver-habit is dragging us down to the demnition bow-wows, another that only an heroic dose of white dollars will save us from industrial death. Political claptrap to corral the succulent pie—"issues" to get office. We have had high and low tariff, the gold and silver standard, greenbackism and "wild-cat" currency; we have had presidents of all shades of political faith and congresses of every kind of economic folly; yet in a single century America has risen from the poorest of nations to the wealthiest in all the world. True it is that wealth is congested—that willful Waste and woeful Want go hand in hand—that the land is filled with plutocrats and paupers; but this distressing fact is due to the faults of our industrial system itself, and can never be reformed by placing fiddle-strings on the free list or increasing the tariff on toothpicks.

Gall? Ye gods! Look at the platform promises of the blessed Democratic party—then at its performances! Look at the party itself—a veritable omnium-gatherum of political odds and ends, huddled together under the party blanket like household gods and barnyard refuse after a hurricane. High and low tariffs and free-traders; gold-bugs, greenbackers and bi-metallists; Cleveland and Croker, Altgeld and Olney, Hill and Hogg, Waco's Warwick and Colonel Culberson's kid, all clamoring to be dyed-in-the-wool Democrats! When I get a new main-spring put in my vocabulary I'm going to tackle the Gall of the Populists and Republicans.

* * *

Some specimens of Gall amaze me by their greatness, some amuse me, while others only spoil my appetite. Of the latter class is the chronic kicker who is forever fuming about feminine fashions. If the hoop-skirt comes in this critic is in agony; if the "pull-back" makes its appearance he has a fit and falls in it. Ever since Eve attired herself in a few freckles and fig-leaves he's been reforming the fashions. Don't mind him, ladies. Like a peacock crying in the night, he's disagreeable, but not dangerous. Adorn yourselves as you see fit; follow such fashions as seem good in your sight, and have no fear that the sons of men will ever forsake you because of your clothes . When you find a man dictating to the ladies what they shall wear you're pretty apt to see his head housed in a stove-pipe hat—the most inartistic and awkward monstrosity ever designed by the devil to make the Almighty ashamed of his masterpiece. In all history there's no record of a great idea being born in a beegum. I never saw a statue of a hero or picture of a martyr with a plug hat on. Imagine the Lord laying aside a silk cady preparatory to preaching that Sermon on the Mount—or Napoleon apostrophizing the pyramids in a plug! Before finding fault with the fashions of the ladies just imagine Apollo in the make-up of a modern society swell, loafing into court on High Olympus! Why Jove would hit him with a thunderbolt so hard there'd be nothing left of him but a wilted chrysanthemum and a pair o' yaller shoes!

* * *

For a specimen of Gall that must amaze the very gods commend me to a crowd of pharisaical plutocrats, piously offering, in a hundred thousand dollar church, prayers to him who had nowhere to lay his head; who pay a preacher $15,000 per annum to point the way to Paradise, while in the great cities of every Christian country children must steal or starve and women choose between death and dishonor. New York is crowded with costly churches that lift their proud spires into the empyrean, that part the clouds with golden fingers—monuments which Mammon rears as if to mock the lowly Son of God. Their value mounts up into the millions; yet I learn—from a religious paper, mark you—that 100,000 men, women and children were evicted in New York alone last year for the non-payment of rent; turned into the streets to suffer summer's heat or winter's cold—to beg, or starve, or steal, as they saw fit. I find these startling statistics in the same column with a tearful appeal for more money to send missionaries to black barbarians—on the same page with a description of a new church that must have cost a cold half-million of cash. That's what I call sanctified assurance—gall masquerading as grace. And what is true of New York is true, in greater or less degree, of every town from Plymouth Rock to Poker Flats, from Tadmor-in-the-Wilderness to Yuba Dam. Everywhere the widow is battling with want, while we send Bibles and blankets, prayer-books and pie, salvation and missionary soup to a job-lot of lazy niggers whose souls aren't worth a soumarkee in blocks-of-five—who wouldn't walk into heaven if the gates were wide open, but once inside would steal the eternal throne if it wasn't spiked down. Let the heathen rage; we've got our hands full at home. I'd rather see the whole black-and-tan aggregation short on Bibles than one white child crying for bread.

While Europe and America are peddling saving grace in pagan lands—and incidentally extending the market for their cheap tobacco, snide jewelry and forty-rod bug-juice—they are also building warships and casting cannon—preparing to cut each others throats while prating of the prince of peace! The idea of countries that have to build forts on their frontiers and keep colossal standing armies to avoid being butchered by their own Christian brethren; that are full of divorce courts and demagogues, penitentiaries and poorhouses, sending young theological goslings, who believe that all of divine revelation can be found in one bok, to teach the philosophic Hindu the road to heaven! Gall! Why the men we are trying to convert were preaching the immortality of the soul when the Hebrew prophets were putting people to the sword for accepting it; they were familiar with all the essential features of the Christian faith a thousand years before the crucifixion of Christ. Charity begins at home. In our own country children are coming up in ignorance and crime, while sect vies with sect in the erection of proud temples in which polite society may display its Parisian finery while pretending to worship One who broke bread with beggars and slept in the brush.

I haven't much use for gold-plated godliness. Christ never built a church, or asked for a vacation on full pay,—never. He indulged in no political harangues—never told his parishioners how to vote—never posed as a professional Prohibitionist. He didn't try to reform the fallen women of Jerusalem by turning them over to the police, a la Parkhurst. Although gladitorial shows were common in his country—and that without gloves—he didn't go raging up and down the earth like some of our Texas dominies, demanding that these awful crimes against civilization should cease. There is no record of his engineering a boycott against business men who dissented from his doctrine. I think he could have read a copy of the Iconoclast with far more patience than some of his successors. Human or divine, he was the grandest man that ever graced the mighty tide of time. His was a labor of love, instead of for lucre. The groves were his temples, the mountain-side his pulpit, the desert his sacristy and Jordan his baptismal font.

* * *

Then there's the unconscious Gall of the pious parrot who is quite sure that the only highway to the heavenly hereafter is outlined by his little sect, macadamized by his creed; that you've got to travel that or get into trouble, perhaps fall into the fire.

Just imagine that dear Lord, who so loved sinners that he died to save them from death eternal, looking over heaven's holy battlements and observing a miserable mortal plunging downward to his doom, leaving behind him a streak of fire like a falling star, his face distorted with fear, his every hair erect and singing like a jewsharp. He asks St. Peter:

"Who's that?"

"Oh," says the man on the door, "that's old John Smith."

The Lord goes over to the office of the Recording Angel and turns the leaves of the great ledger. He finds the name, "John Smith, No. 11027," and on the credit page these entries: "He was fearless as Caesar, generous as Macaenas, tender as Gautama and true to his friends as the stars to their appointed courses. He was a knight of nature's nobility, a lord in the aristocracy of intellect, courtier at home and a king abroad. On the debit page he reads: "Went fishing on Sunday. There was a miscue on his baptism. He knew a pretty woman from an ancient painting, a jack-pot from a prayer-book, and when smitten on one cheek he made the smacker think he'd been smuck by a cyclone." Good-bye, John!

It may be that the monarch of the majestic universe marches around after every inconsequential little mortal, note-book in hand, giving him a white mark when he prays for the neighbor who poisons his dog, or tells his wife the truth regardless of consequences; a black one when he bets his money on the wrong horse or sits down on the sidewalk and tries to swipe the front gate as it goes sailing by; but I doubt it. If I could make the sun, moon and stars in one day and build a beautiful woman of an old bone, I'd just like to see the color of that man's hair I'd waste much time and attention on.

* * *

Why should we quarrel about our faiths and declare that this is right and that is wrong, when all religions are, and must of necessity ever be, fundamentally one and the same—the worship of a superior power, the great

> "Father of all, in every age, in ev'ry clime adored,
> By saint, by savage and by sage, Jehovah, Jove, or Lord."

* * *

Man's cool assumption that the Almighty made him as his "masterpiece" should be marked Exhibit A in the mighty aggregation of Gall. That after millions of years experience in the creation business—after building the arch-angels and the devil; after making the man in the moon and performing other wondrous miracles, the straddling six-foot biped who wears a spike-tail coat and plug hat, a silk surcingle and sooner tie; who parts his name on the side and his hair in the middle; who sucks a cane and simpers like a school-girl struggling with her first compliment; who takes it for granted that he knows it all, when his whole life—including his birth, marriage and death—is a piece of ridiculous guess-work; who insists that he has a soul to save, yet labors with might and main to lose it; protests that there's a better land beyond the grave, yet moves heaven and earth to keep from going to it so long as he can help it—the assumption, I say, that this was the best the Creator could do, is *prima facie* evidence of a plentitude of Gall of the purest ray serene.

The calm assurance of man that the earth and all it contains were made for his especial benefit; that woman was created solely for his comfort; that the sun was made to give him light by day and the moon to enable him to find his way home from the lodge at night without the aid of a policeman; that the heavens were hung with a resplendent curtain of stars and the planets sent whirling thro' space in a majestic dance about the God of Day, simply to afford him matter for wonder or for amusement when too tired to talk politics or too bilious to drink beer, evinces an egotism that must amuse the Almighty.

Masterpiece indeed! Why, God made man, and, finding that he couldn't take care of himself, made woman to take care of him—and she proposes to discharge her heaven-ordained duty or know the reason why. Tennyson says that, "as the husband is the wife is;" but even Tennyson didn't know it quite all. When wives take their hubbies for measures of morality, marriage will become an enthusiastic failure and Satan be loosed for a little season. We acknowledge woman's superiority by demanding that she be better than we could if we would, or would be if we could.

We are fond of alluding to woman as "the weaker vessel;" but she can *break* the best of us if given an opportunity. Pope calls man the "great lord of all things"—but Pope never got married. We rule with a rod of iron the creatures of the earth and air and sea; we hurl our withering defi in the face of Kings and brave presidential lightning; we found empires and straddle the perilous political issue, then surrender unconditionally to a little bundle of dimples and deviltry, sunshine and extravagance. No man ever followed freedom's flag for patriotism (and a pension) with half the enthusiasm that he will trail the red, white and blue that constitute the banner of female beauty. The monarch's fetters cannot curtail our haughty freedom, nor nature's majestic forces confine us to this little lump of clay; we tread the ocean's foam beneath our feet, harness the thunderbolts of imperial Jove to the jaunting car, and even aspire to mount the storm and walk upon the wind; yet the bravest of us tremble like cowards and lie like Cretans when called to account by our wives for some of our cussedness.

But you will say that I have wandered from my text—have followed the ladies off and got lost. Well, it's not the first time it's happened. But really, I'm not so inconsistent as I may seem; for if the gentler sex exceeds us in goodness it likewise surpasses us in Gall. Perhaps the most colossal exhibit of polite and elegant audacity this world can boast is furnished by that female who has made a *marriage of convenience;* has wedded money instead of a man,—practically put her charms up at auction for the highest bidder—yet who poses as a paragon of purity; gathers up her silken skirts—the price of her legalized shame—lest they come in contact with the calico gown of some poor girl who has loved, not wisely, but too well.

Marriage is the most sacred institution ever established on earth, making the father, mother and child a veritable Holy Trinity; but it is rapidly degenerating into an unclean Humbug, in which Greed is God and Gall is recognized high priest. We now consider our fortunes rather than our affections, acquire a husband or wife much as we would a parrot or a poodle, and get rid of them with about as little compunction. Cupid now feathers his arrows from the wings of the gold eagle and shoots at the stomach instead of the heart. Love without law makes angels blush; but law without love crimsons even the brazen bow of infamy.

* * *

But the fact that so many selfish, soulless marriages are made is not altogether woman's fault. Our ridiculous social code is calculated to crush all sentiment and sweetness out of the gentler sex—to make woman regard herself as merchandise rather than as a moral entity, entitled to life, liberty and the pursuit of happiness. The average woman must select a husband from a narrow circle; must make choice among two or three admirers or elect to live a loveless old maid—to forego the joys of motherhood, the happiness of a home. Man is privileged to go forth and seek a mate. The world is before him, a veritable "Dream of Fair Women." He wanders at will, as amid a mighty parterre of flowers, sweet as the breath of morn, and finally, before some fair blossom he bows the knee—pours forth the incense of his soul to the one woman in all the world he would make his wife. True, she may refuse him and marry some other fellow; but he is at least privileged to approach her, to plead his cause, to employ all the art and eloquence of love to bring her into his life. Woman enjoys no such privilege. She must wait to be wooed, and if her king comes not she must take the best that offers and try to be content.

Every daughter of Eve dreams of an ideal,—of a man tender and true, who will fill her life with love's own melody; his word her law, his home her heaven, his honor her glory and his tomb her grave. And some day, from these castles in the clouds he comes—these day-dreams, golden as the dawn, become the halo of a mortal man, to whom her heart turns as the helianthus to the sun. At last the god of her idolatry doth walk the earth; but she must stand afar,—must not, by word or act, betray the holy passion that's consuming her, lest "that monster custom, of habits devil," doth brand her bold and bad. Love ofttimes begets love, as the steel strikes fire from the cold flint, and a word from her might bring him to her feet; but she must stand with dumb lips and assumed indifference and see him drift out of her life, leaving it desolate as the Scythian desert, when it should have budded and blossomed like the great blush rose. So she drifts desolate into old maidenhood and the company of Maltese cats; else, when hope is dead in her heart—when the dream of her youth has become dust and ashes—she marries for money and tries to feed her famished heart with Parisian finery, to satisfy her soul with the Dead Sea fruit of fashion.

No; I wouldn't give woman the ballot—not in a thousand years. I want no petticoats in politics—no she-senators or female presidents; but I'd do better by woman; I'd repeal that ridiculous social law—survival of female slavery—which compels her to wait to be wooed. I'd put a hundred leap-years in every century, give woman the right to do half the courting—to find a man to her liking and capture him if she could. Talk about reforms! Why, the bachelors would simply have to become Benedicts or take to the brush, and there'd be no old maids outside the dime museums. But I was speaking of Gall.

* * *

Gall is usually unadulterated impudence; but sometimes it is irremediably idiocy. When you find a man pluming himself on his ancestors you can safely set it down that he's got the disease in its latter form, and got it bad. I always feel sorry for a man who's got nothing to be proud of but a dead gran'-daddy, for it appears to be a law of nature that there shall be but one great man to a tribe—that the lightning of genius shall not twice strike the same family tree. I suppose that Cleveland and Jim Corbett, Luther and Mrs. Lease, Homer and J. S. Hogg had parents and gran-parents; but we don't hear much about 'em. And while the ancestors of the truly great are usually lost in the obscurity of the cornfield or cotton patch, their children seldom succeed in setting the world on fire. Talent may be transmitted from father to son; but you can no more inherit genius than you can inherit a fall out of a balloon. It is the direct gift of that God who is no respecter of persons, and who sheds his glory on the cotter's child as freely as on those of monarchs and of millionaires.

We have in this country three aristocracies: The aristocracy of intellect, founded by the Almighty; the aristocracy of money, founded by Mammon, and the aristocracy of family, founded by fools. The aristocracy of brains differs from those of birth and boodle as a star differs from a jack-o'-lantern, as the music of the spheres from the bray of a burro, as a woman's first love from the stale affection hashed up for a fourth husband.

To the aristocracy of money belong many worthy men; but why should the spirit of mortal be proud? The founder of one of the wealthiest and most exclusive of American families skinned beeves and made weinerwurst. The calling was an honest and useful one. His sausages were said to be excellent, and at a *skin* game he was exceptionally hard to beat; but his descendants positively decline to put a calf's head regardant and a cleaver rampant on their coat-of-arms. A relative much addicted to the genealogical habit once assured me that he could trace our family back 600 years just as easy as following the path to the drugstore in a Prohibition town. I was delighted to hear it, to learn that I too had ancestors—that some of them were actually on the earth before I was born. While he was tracing I was figuring. I found that in 600 years there should be 20 generations—if everybody did his duty—and that in 20 generations a man has 2,093,056 ancestors! Just think of it! Why, if he had gone back 600 years further he might have discovered that I was a lineal descendant of Adam, perhaps distantly related to crowned monarchs—if not to the Duke of Marlborough. As my cousin couldn't account for this job-lot of kinsmen—had no idea how many had been hanged, gone into politics or written poetry, I rang him off. Those people who delight to trace their lineage through several generations to some distinguished man should be tapped for the simples. When

John Smith starts out to found a family and marries Miss Jones, their son is half Smith and half Jones. The next crop is nearly one-fourth Smith and at the end of a dozen generations the young Smiths bear about as much relation to the original as they do to a rabbit.

* * *

There are various grades of Gall; but perhaps the superlative brand is that which leads a man to look down with lofty scorn upon those of his fellow mortals who have tripped on Life's rugged pathway and plunged into a shoreless sea of shame. I am no apologist for crime—I would not cover its naked hideousness with the Arachne-robe of sentiment; but I do believe that many a social outcast, many a branded criminal, will get as sweet a harp in the great hereafter as those who have kept themselves unspotted from the world. It is easy enough to say grace over a good square meal, to be honest on a fat income, to praise God when full of pie; but just wait till you get the same razzle-dazzle the devil dished up for Job and see how your halle-hallelujahs hold out before exalting your horn. Victory does not always proclaim the hero nor virtue the saint. It were easy enough to sail with wind and tide—to float over fair seas, mid purple isles of spice; but the captain who loses his ship mid tempests dire, mid wreck and wrath, may be a better sailor and a braver than the master who rides safe to port with rigging all intact and every ensign flying. With

> "The boast of heraldry, the pomp of power,
> And all that beauty, all that wealth e'er gave,"

it were easy enough to be a good citizen and a consistent Christian. It is poverty and contempt, suffering and disappointment that try men's souls—that proclaim of what metal they are made. Faith, Hope and Charity are man's triune transcendent—"and the greatest of these is Charity." A pharisee is either a pious fraud or a hopeless fool—he's either short on "gumption" or long on Gall.

* * *

Half the alleged honesty of this world is but Gall, and must be particularly offensive to the Almighty. We have oodles of men in every community who are legally honest, but morally rotten. Legal honesty is the brand usually proclaimed as "the best policy." Only fools risk the penitentiary to fill their purse. The smart rogue is ever "honest within the law"—infamous in strict accord with the criminal code.

Dives may attire himself in purple and fine linen and fare sumptuously every day, while Lazarus lies at his door for the dogs to lick, vainly craving the crumbs that fall from the millionaire's table, and still be legally honest, even a church member in good standing; but his loyalty to legal forms will avail him but little when he finds his coat-tails afire and no water within forty miles.

The girl who flirts with a featherless young gosling till he doesn't know whether he's floating in a sea of champagne to the sound of celestial music, sliding down a greased rainbow or riding on the ridge-pole of the aurora borealis, then tells him that she can only be a kind of Christmas-present, opera-ticket sister to him; who steals his unripe affections and allows 'em to get frostbitten—carries him into the empyrean of puppy-love, only to drop him with a dull plunk that fills his callow heart with compound fractures—well, she cannot be prosecuted for petit larceny nor indicted for malicious mischief; but the unfortunate fellow who finally gets her will be glad to go to heaven, where there's neither marrying or giving in marriage.

The man who preaches Prohibition in public and pays court to a gallon jug of corn-juice in private; who damns the saloon at home and sits up with it all night abroad, may not transcend the law of the land, but if his Gall should burst the very buzzards would break their necks trying to get out of the country

The druggist who charges a poor dunderhead a dollar foı filling a prescription that calls in Latin for a spoonful of salt and an ounce of water, may do no violence to the criminal code, but he plays ducks and drakes with the moral law.

The little tin-horn attorney, whose specialties are divorce cases and libel suits; who stirs up good-for-naughts to sue publishers for $10,000 damages to 10-cent reputations; who's as ready to shield Vice from the sword of Justice as to defend Virtue from stupid violence; who's ever for sale to the highest bidder and keeps eloquence on tap for whosoever cares to buy; who would rob the orphan of his patrimony on a technicality or brand the Virgin Mary as a bawd to shield a black-mailer—well, he cannot be put into the penitentiary, more's the pity! but it's some satisfaction to believe that, if in all the great universe of God there is a hell where fiends lie howling, the most sulphurous section is reserved for the infamous shyster—that if he cannot be debarred from the courts of earth he'll get the bounce from those of heaven.

The woman who inveigles some poor fool—perhaps old

enough to be her father—into calling her his tootsie-wootsie over his own signature, then brings suit for breach of promise—or the Seventh Commandment; who exhibits her broken heart to the judge and jury and demands that it be patched up with Uncle Sam's illuminated anguish plasters; who plays the adventuress, then poses in the public prints as an injured innocent—sends a good reputation to join a bad character in hope of monetary reward—well, she too may be legally honest; but it's just as well to watch her, for no woman worth powder to blow her to perdition ever did or ever will carry such a case into court. When a woman's heart is really hurting her money is not going to help it; when she's truly sorry for her sin she tells her troubles to the Lord instead of to policemen and reporters.

The man who sues a fellow-citizen for alienating his wife's affections, instead of striking his trail with a bell-mouthed blunderbuss and a muzzle-loading bulldog; who asks the court to put a silver lining into the cloud of infamy that hangs over his home; who tries to make capital of his shame and heal with golden guineas the hurt that honor feels—well, he too may be a law-abiding citizen; but ten thousand such souls, if separated from their Gall, might play hide-and-seek on the surface of a copper cent for a hundred years and never find each other.

* * *

Dignity is but a peculiar manifestation of Gall. It is the stock in trade of fools. If Almighty God ever put up great dignity and superior intellect in the same package it must have got misplaced. They are opposing elements, as antagonistic as the doctrines of infinite love and infant damnation. Knowledge makes men humble; true genius is ever modest. The donkey is popularly supposed to be the most stupid animal extant—excepting the dude. He's also the most dignified—since the extinction of the dodo. No pope or president, rich in the world's respect; no prince or potentate reveling in the pride of sovereign power; no poet or philosopher bearing his blushing honors thick upon him ever equaled a blind donkey in impressive dignity. As a man's vision broadens; as he begins to realize what a miserable little microbe he is in that mighty immensity, studded with the stupendous handiwork of a power that transcends his comprehension, his dignity drains off and he feels like asking to be recognized just long enough to apologize for his existence.

When I see a little man strut forth in the face of heaven like a turkey-cock on dress parade; forgotten aeons behind him, blank time before him, his birth a mystery, his death a leap in the dark; when I see him pose on the grave of forgotten races and puff himself up with pomposity like the frog in the fable; when I see him sprinkled with the dust of fallen dynasties and erecting new altars upon the site of forgotten fanes, yet staggering about under a load of dignity that would spring the knee-joints of an arch-angel, I don't wonder that the Lord once decided to drown the whole layout like a litter of blind puppies.

* * *

A lecture on Gall were woefully incomplete without some reference to the press, that "archimedean lever" and "moulder of public opinion." The average newspaper posing as a "public educator" is a specimen of Gall that cannot be properly analyzed in one evening. Men do not establish newspapers for the express purpose of reforming the world, but rather to print what a large number of people in a particular community want to read and are willing to pay for. A newspaper is simply a mirror in which the community sees itself, not as it should be, but as it actually is. It is not the mother, but the daughter of public opinion. The printing press is a mighty phonograph that echoes back the joy and the sorrow, the glory and the shame of the generation it serves. I have no more quarrel with editors for filling their columns with inanities than casting shadows when they stand in the sun. They know what kind of mental pabulum their people crave, and they are no more in business for their health than is the merchant. They know that should they print the grandest sermon that ever fell from Massillon's lips of gold not 20 per cent, even of the professedly pious, would read it; but that a detailed account of a fragrant divorce case or international prizefight will cause 99 per cent of the very elect of the Lord to swoop down upon it like a hungry hen-hawk on an unripe gosling and fairly devour it, then roll their eyes to heaven like a calf with the colic and wonder what this wicked old world is coming to. The editor knows that half the people who pretend to be filled to overflowing with the grace of God are only perambulating pillars of pure Gall. He knows that the very people who criticise him for printing accounts of crimes and making spreads on sporting events, would transfer their patronage to other papers if he heeded their howling—that they are talking for effect thro' the crown of their felts.

Speaking of prizefights reminds me that a governor who, after winking at a hundred brutal slugging matches, puts his state to the expense of a legislative session to prevent a pair of gladiators pounding each other with soft gloves, is not suffering for lack of Gall; that those pious souls who never suspected that pugilism was an insult to our civilization until they got a good opportunity to make a grandstand play, then whereased and resoluted themselves black in the face anent its brutality, should be presented with a medal of pure brass. Politics is said to make strange bedfellows, but I scarce expected to see a shoestring gambler and would-be Don Juan lauded by ministerial associations as "our heroic young Christian governor."

Gall? Why, Geo. Clark presumes to give Bismarck pointers and congress advice. Nobody knows so well how to manage a husband as an old maid. A bachelor can give the father of a village pointers on the training of boys. Our Northern neighbors know exactly how to deal with the nigger. The man who would starve but for the industry of his wife feels competent to manage the finances of the country. People who couldn't be trusted to wean a calf, tell us all about the Creator of the Cosmos. Sam Jones wants to debate with Bob Ingersoll, and every forks-of-the-creek economist takes a hard fall out of Henry George. The A. P. A. agitators prate loudly of freedom of conscience and insist on disfranchising the Catholics. We boast of religious liberty, then enact iron-clad Sunday laws that compel Jew and pagan to conform to our creed or go to prison. The prohibs want to confine the whole world to cold water because their leaders haven't sufficient stamina to stay sober. Men who fail to make a living at honest labor insist on entering the public service. Political parties charge up to each other the adverse decrees of Providence. Atheists deny the existence of God because he doesn't move in their set, while ministers assume that a criticism of themselves is an insult to the Creator.

* * *

But to detain you longer were to give a practical illustration of my text. I will be told that Gall is a necessary evil; that a certain amount of audacity, of native impudence, is necessary to success. I deny it. Fame and wealth and power constitute our ideal of success—folly born of falsehood. Only the useful are successful. Father Damien was the grandest success of the century; Alexander of Macedon the most miserable failure known to human history—with the possible exception of Grover Cleveland. Alexander employed his genius to conquer the Orient and Cleveland his stupidity to ruin the Occident. The kingdom of the one went to pieces, and the party of the other is now posing as the lost tribe of the political Israel!

Success? A Gould must give up his gold at the grave, the

sovereign surrender his sceptre, the very gods are in time forgotten—are swallowed up in the voiceless, viewless past, hidden by the shadows of the centuries. Why should men strive for fame, that feather in the cap of fools, when nations and peoples perish like the flowers and are forgotten—when even continents fade from the great world's face and the ocean's bed becomes the mountain's brow. Why strive for power, that passes like the perfume of the dawn, and leaves prince and pauper peers in death? Why should man, made in the mortal image of immortal God, become the subservient slave of Greed and barter all of time for a handful of yellow dross to cast upon the threshold of eternity? "Poor and content is rich," and rich enough. With a roof to shelter those his heart holds dear, and table furnished forth with frugal fare; with manhood's dauntless courage and woman's deathless love, the peasant in his lowly cot may be richer far than the prince in his imperial hall.

Success? I would rather be a fox and steal fat geese than a miserly millionaire and prey upon the misfortunes of my fellows. I would rather be a doodle-bug burrowing in the dust than a plotting politician, trying to inflate a second-term gubernatorial boom with the fetid breath of a foul hypocrisy. I would rather be a peddler of hot peanuts than a President who gives to bond-grabbers and boodlers privilege to despoil the pantries of the poor. I would rather be a louse on the head of a lazar than lord high executioner of a theological college that, to preserve its reputation and fill its coffers with filthy lucre, brands an orphan babe as a bawd. I would rather watch the stars shining down thro' blue immensity, and the cool mists creeping round the purple hills, than feast my eyes on all the tawdry treasures of Ophir and of Ind. I would rather play a corn-stalk fiddle while pickaninnies dance, than build, of widows' sighs and orphans' tears, a flimsy bubble of fame to be blown adown the narrow beach of Time into Eternity's shoreless sea. I would rather be the beggar lord of a lodge in the wilderness, dress in a suit of sunburn and live on hominy and hope, yet see the love-light blaze unbought in truthful eyes, than to be the marauding emperor of the mighty world, and know not who fawned upon the master and who esteemed the man.

IMMORTALITY

Brann belonged to no church, and was often called an atheist. He was more properly a deist, as evidenced by this brief, revealing essay.

I know nothing of the future; I spend no time speculating upon it—I am overwhelmed by the Past and at death-grips with the Present. At the grave God draws the line between the two eternities. Never has living man lifted the sombre veil of Death and looked beyond. "Revealed Religion" was not born of Reason or nursed by Knowledge; it is the child of Love and Pain, and lives between the rosy breasts of Hope.

There is a Deity. I have felt His presence, I have heard His voice, I have been cradled in His imperial robe. All that is, or was, or can be, is but "the visible garment of God." I ask no written covenant with God, for He is my Father. I will trust Him without requiring priests or prophets to endorse His note. As I write my little son awakes, alarmed by some noise, and comes groping through the darkness to my door. He sees the light shining through the transom, returns to his trundle-bed and lies down to peaceful dreams. He knows that beyond that gleam his father keeps watch and ward, and he asks no more. Through a thousand celestial transoms streams the light of God. Why should I fear the sleep of Death, the unknown terrors of that starless night, the waves of the River Styx? Why should I seek assurance from the lips of men that the wisdom, love and power of my heavenly Father will not fail?

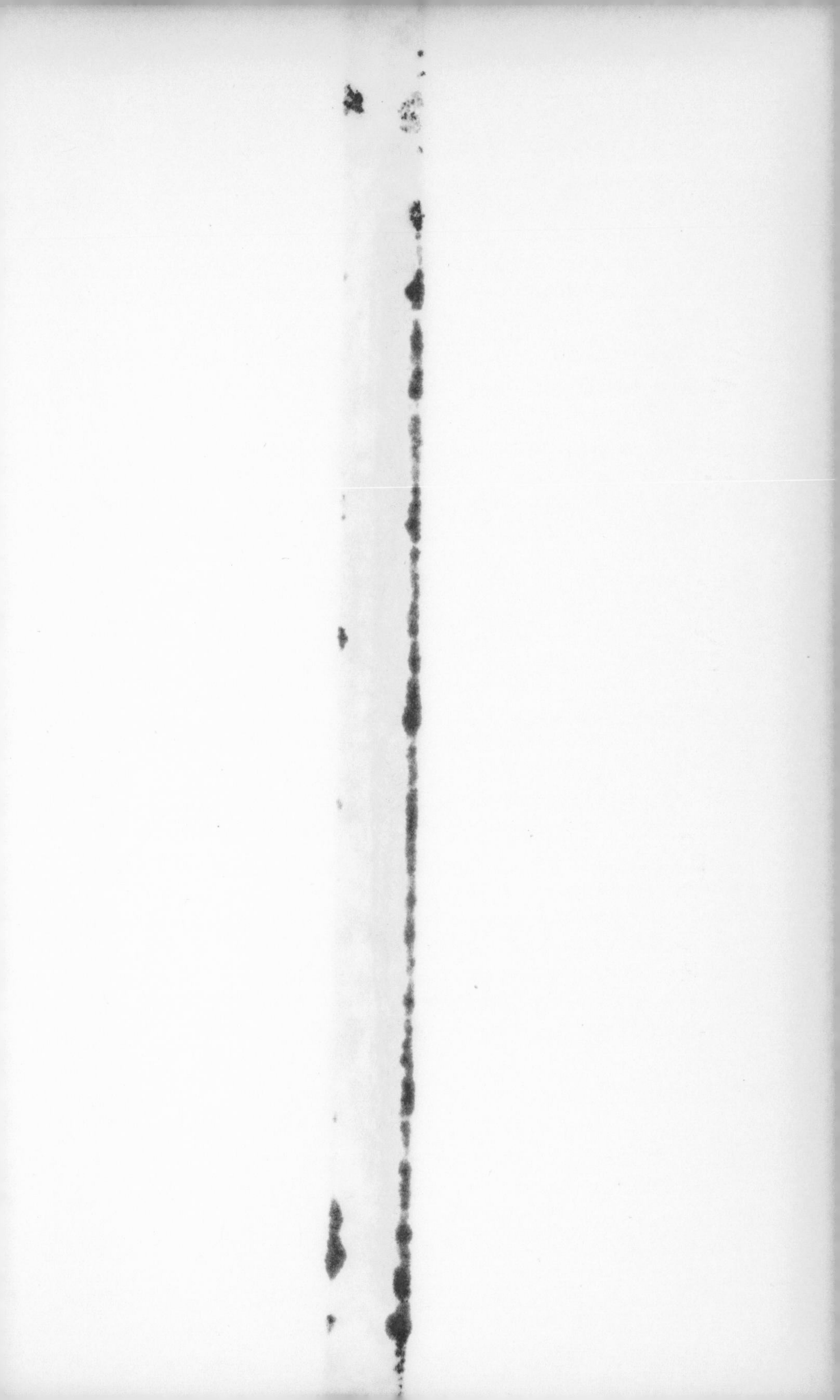

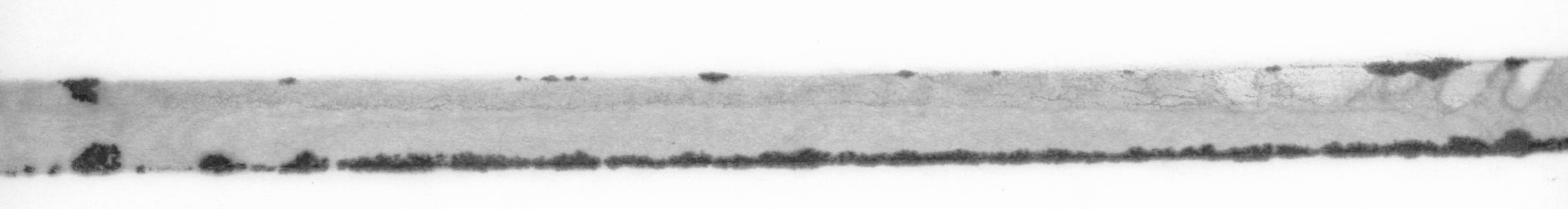